4/21/06

Jimmy,

We're reading this wave together!
I love you
Linda

RIDE THE WAVE OF CHANGE

THE ULTIMATE GUIDE TO LIFE SURFING

BY

NORMAN MITCHELL, PH. D.

authorHOUSE™

1663 LIBERTY DRIVE, SUITE 200
BLOOMINGTON, INDIANA 47403
(800) 839-8640
WWW.AUTHORHOUSE.COM

First published by AuthorHouse 10/28/05

ISBN: 1-4208-6382-7 (sc)

Library of Congress Control Number: 2005905420

Printed in the United States of America
Bloomington, Indiana

This book is printed on acid-free paper.

TABLE OF CONTENTS

This book is dedicated to everyone who brings light into our ever darkening world.

Acknowledgments

It is so difficult to remember all the friends and colleagues who have helped me along my long journey to shape the Life Surfing concept. Nevertheless, I'd like to try.

First and foremost this book would never have been published without the love, support, and brutal honesty from my best friend and wife, Deb.

I am thankful for the honor and the opportunity to be touched by the lives of so many participants through the years in all my training courses presented at Core States Bank, Vanguard Cellular Systems, AT&T Wireless Services, and Harley-Davidson Motor Company. I can't forget my ex-partners Carl Wagner and Michelle Rix and everyone from the Life Nourishment Center.

Finally I want to thank Randy Shackelford, Margaret Mohr, Dr. Marilyn Lutz, Dr. Charlie Kupfer, Anne Atwell, Cathy Sumner, Sandy Nevius, Larry Arnold, Rev, Dr. Stephen Gallaher, and Carolyn Hill for their input and their time invested in reading and editing my manuscript.

INTRODUCTION

From a very young age, I have always wanted to help people, although as a child and then a teenager, I was never clear on how I would do this. What I did know was that I was fascinated by people. While growing up, some of my friends liked to take clocks, radios, and the like apart to figure out what made them work. I enjoyed doing that with people. I enjoyed mentally watching and analyzing the behaviors of people around me to see how they reacted in particular situations. I considered myself then—and still do today—a people watcher. In spite of everything that has occurred in my life, it remains intriguing the way people behave and respond to situations in their lives.

This fascination, which as an adult I realized was the study of human behavior, was the testing ground for this book. Through the years, I have been on a quest to help me understand what makes people tick. I have been a student of life, studying both formally and informally for more insight. My path has taken me in many directions, and fortunately in a direction where I could help others.

I am by no means an authority on living a life devoid of stress, chaos, and hardship; I do not consider myself smarter than most people or special in any way. What I have been able to do is develop a career in corporate training and organizational development where I could use my knowledge of human nature to provide skills for people that enabled them to cope better with their life situations and remain more balanced in times of uncertainty.

These skills are a composite of many years of research and study in psychology, philosophy, Eastern religions, physics, metaphysics and new age methodologies. They are an eclectic blend that I have woven together to form the basis of what I call Life Surfing."

I chose the title *The Ultimate Guide for Life Surfing* because of the similarities between the skills used for ocean surfing and the skills we use to manage our lives. Not only is ocean surfing a sport, but for millions, a way of life. I use it as an analogy because ocean surfing incorporates the physical, mental, and emotional toughness that transcends the sport itself. Ocean surfers have this certain sense about them that creates their passion to challenge the ocean and ride its waves. The analogy is a perfect fit because it compares the dispositions of surfers and the cyclical nature of waves in the ocean with what it takes to successfully ride the waves of change and uncertainty in our lives.

Ocean surfers blend strong mental concentration with physical dexterity to strive to become "one" with the wave. They combine incredible strength and balance with a laid-back attitude that lets them forget their wipeouts and look forward to riding the next wave. The thrill is in the ride as they mold themselves into the wave and generate the flexibility, responsiveness, and courage to accept whatever the wave gives them. In an instant, not only are they able to fling their arms and gyrate their torsos to avert an impending fall, but they make it look effortless!

This mentality of ocean surfing, when applied to our everyday lives, affords us the opportunity to learn how to face life's unexpected changes and uncertainties with a sense of balance born from optimism and confidence. This mentality is the true essence of Life Surfing."

Ocean surfers prepare themselves to understand that at any given moment, the ocean can become hazardous or gentle, and to always keep their eyes on the ocean. Life surfers prepare themselves to realize that at any given moment, life will present unexpected twists and turns, and have developed the physical, mental, and emotional fortitude to stay strong when the unexpected occurs.

To an ocean surfer, no wave is the same. Although waves may look alike, they each have their own identity. One ocean surfer will ride the same wave differently than another ocean surfer. In our daily lives, every day is different. One person handles day-to-day change differently than another. No ocean wave is separate from another, because they are all connected in a cycle of perpetual motion. The waves of change and uncertainty in our lives are also connected in a similar sense of perpetual motion, because they have a ripple effect, creating numerous waves that alter multiple events in our lives.

Some waves that ocean surfers see coming are higher than others, and offer more danger for them. Aware of the danger, they still paddle out to meet the challenge. Some waves appear without notice and are upon ocean surfers before they have a chance to react. Modern-day ocean surfers have adapted and maintain their edge by using smaller and lighter boards to attack and slash their way through the waves.

Some waves of change and uncertainty in our lives we see and others we don't. Life surfers know that changes are never identically the same, and have become more adept at keeping their edge by adapting to and coping with the rolling waves of change in their daily lives.

Ocean surfers understand the danger and know that the next wave could be their last. The waves and tides of the ocean are unpredictable, yet ocean surfers do not let this interfere with their passion to surf. Life surfers face change and uncertainty with a similar sense of passion and excitement.

Ocean surfing is and will always be an exciting sport, due to the exhilaration felt while standing on a surfboard, riding the waves of the ocean. In 1907, George Freeth came to Redondo Beach, California from Hawaii to demonstrate surfing as a publicity stunt to promote the opening of the Redondo-Los Angeles railroad owned by Henry Huntington. Freeth stayed in California, became a lifeguard, and introduced ocean surfing to the United States.

In the early 1950s, ocean surfing became quite popular along California beaches from Santa Barbara to San Diego. Surfboard manufacturers began promoting ocean surfing and mass producing boards. In the late '50s, boards made of resin and setting fluids set the sport booming. The budding sport gave birth to a new musical style, the screaming reverb guitar sound.

Beach movies, surfing magazines, and surf songs were the rage in the '60s. Flowered and art deco shirts, baggy surf swim trunks, sandals, and faded Levi''s became an accepted fashion mode. There was intense interest in this new surfing culture as it spread across America. Since then, ocean surfing has influenced our fashion, language, and sporting activities through the world. Ocean surfing is much more than a sport; it is a way of life.

I have integrated the concepts of ocean surfing to create Life Surfing, which after twenty-five years of teaching workshops, seminars, and corporate training classes, has proven invaluable to address stress, change, and crisis management. I have personally used and continue to use the techniques and exercises provided within this book, and they continue to change my life for the better. I wrote this book to respond to the many requests I received from participants in my professional courses and work over many years.

The Ultimate Guide to Life Surfing will teach you how to become a life surfer by using practical techniques to handle both the unexpected (those not chosen) and expected (those chosen) changes in your life.

Briefly, the book has three basic sections:

1. The first six chapters present the basic concepts used to build Life Surfing skills.

2. The next five chapters define the "CHARM" process, which includes Life Surfing techniques and exercises to keep you in control during times of transition and uncertainty.

3. The last few chapters provide advanced techniques and exercises for remaining positive when life gives you the most challenging waves to ride.

This book discusses how change and uncertainty affect you, and the challenges they present. It offers techniques to help you maintain self-control in times of change and uncertainty. This book is a journey consisting of concepts discussed in each chapter that connect as you progress through the book. I start by discussing your natural resistance and fears regarding change and progress by offering insights into gaining confidence and providing techniques for remaining empowered when life becomes chaotic. I offer rapport-building exercises as well as techniques to use when dealing with people who make you nervous, uncomfortable, and anxious.

I'll introduce you to the "CHARM" process, which consists of five components that, when utilized together, enable you to maintain self-control and become flexible to successfully ride through the changes and uncertainty in life that no one can avoid forever. Exercises are offered throughout the book that will help you learn how to become a life surfer as well as enhancing your existing Life Surfing skills.

The best ocean surfers want to be the best and practice to hone their skills. They accept that they must compete against other surfers to prove their merit. The exercises in this book teach you new skills for riding the waves of change and uncertainty in your life, to enhance your Life Surfing skills. You will need to practice them if you want to be a successful life surfer.

To augment your development, I provide techniques that will keep you remain positive during times of uncertainty and help you recover from the waves of change that may cause devastation.

At the end of each chapter, I summarize some key points from the material in that chapter and present them from the perspective of Life Surfing, as well as offering quotes to motivate and to inspire you. All the exercises in the book are chronologically listed in the appendix for quick viewing. There is also a bibliography with resources I used for this book that include additional reading for your continued development.

Before you begin this book, let me state that change is a cycle of constant motion. The only true certainty is that change, like the waves in the ocean, will continue to roll into our lives. There is much we can learn from ocean surfing to help us maintain our balance as we manage change and uncertainty in our lives. The techniques and exercises provided have the potential to help you become a great life surfer; they will also impact your life in positive ways and influence how you will ride your waves of change forever.

Like the waves in the ocean that never stop rolling in, so do the waves of change and uncertainty in your life. So, surf's up! Let's begin to learn the art of Life Surfing.

"Commit yourself to work against the forces of negativity by concentrating on your efforts totally towards the creative, positive forces within you." – Norman Mitchell

1. LIFE SURFING

Life Surfing is a set of skills you can apply to help control the forces in your life. I'm sure you are using some of these skills now to cope with the pressures caused by change and uncertainty you are facing in your life. You are not alone if you feel challenged trying to keep up with everything going on in your life. You may have so much to do at work — it is challenging to get it all done by the end of the day. Sometimes you may not even find the time to read, let alone return all your e-mail by the end of your workday.

Everyone seems so busy all the time. The economy has brought hard times for businesses, and although your organization is short-staffed and you feel overwhelmed, you feel lucky to have a job. Therefore, you do the best you can within the restraints of the time and resources you have.

Besides complications at work, you have a personal life too. For some people, it is challenging separating their personal lives from their professional lives. For others, it is balancing quality time between their personal and professional lives.

You may feel as if there is never enough time to get things done. It always seems that there is so much to do. You are forced to neglect some things simply because you do not have the time or energy to do them. You swear you'll get to them later. Maybe you do and maybe you don't.

Your frustration and aggravation level build to the point where you may feel helpless. You have learned to live with this stress and accept it as a way of life. You have reached a point where it is bearable, but it still bothers you.

Life is tough enough to handle, but what happens when a major change occurs? "Oh no," you may think, "how will I manage now?"

Major life changes can include facing health problems, losing your job due to downsizing, going through a divorce, being dumped by a significant other, or constantly feeling underappreciated by others. Perhaps you are a single parent searching for the right relationship, or remarried and raising two sets of children. Regardless, change keeps you wrestling with issues surrounding your money, family, or relationships.

Please don't give up hope. There is a way to manage the complexities of life. Your hope lies in your ability to use Life Surfing skills to help you shift from survival mode (which makes you feel overwhelmed and helpless) and become proactive and take control of your life.

Life surfers adapt the skills used in ocean surfing to help them maintain a balance as they ride the waves of change and uncertainty in their lives. Life surfers embody a combination of freedom and self-determination to help them face the challenges of life. When in the ocean, an ocean surfer needs to be relaxed, as there is no question that the ocean is in charge.

Ocean surfers stay alert at all times. They watch the surf and try to become familiar with it. They learn to understand the different types of waves and how to ride each one. An ocean surfer may sit on the beach, watching for hours before jumping in and riding the waves. An experienced ocean surfer knows the right time to ride and the right time not to ride.

Life surfers can learn from ocean surfers. Life surfers maintain the same sense of confidence and self-direction as they ride the waves of change in their lives. Life surfers always accept that life is bigger than them, and stay relaxed, accepting that life is something they may not be able to control. Just like with ocean surfers, life surfers apply the following skills to help control themselves as they move through the challenges they face in their lives.

Keeping your focus – No matter how challenging or difficult a situation is, it is paramount that you always maintain the direction of your thoughts and feelings. Never let them get the best of you; this opens the door to feeling overwhelmed and helpless.

Avoiding negative patterns – It is so easy to revert to old, negative habits when you are stressed. How can you expect different results when you do the same things over and over again?

Concentrating on where you are going – Challenge yourself to break free from your haunting thoughts and feelings of desperation.

Create a practical, realistic plan and stay determined to follow it.

Using mistakes as learning points – Accept that you will make mistakes. Instead of getting upset, use them as a compass to point you in another direction. Enhancing your Life Surfing skills is a process, not an event, and it takes time.

Knowing how to eliminate unwanted stress – You are holding onto thoughts and emotions that you no longer need. Not only that, but learn that you can't successfully solve problems that are not yours. Stop taking on more than you can handle, and let go of what is excess baggage.

Being flexible – You cannot control everything, and everything will not go as you want. Be ready to adjust to the current of life and be open to go in new directions. Know that at any given moment, things will not remain stable and anything, at any time, could happen. Let go of your attachment to things and keep asking yourself, "What's the worst that could happen?"

Understanding that attitudes are contagious – The way you think, feel, and believe has a direct effect on your behaviors. When you believe you can do something, you will.

Having the courage to pick yourself up and ride another wave – When you fall, get back up. The longer you stay down, the harder it will be to get back up. You are not perfect. You will not succeed every time. Believe that failure is the key to success and without failure there is no success.

Knowing when to ride or coast – Have the conviction to hold your ground and let things evolve before acting. Getting out of the way, at the right time, and not getting involved can be the best move to make.

Recognizing when you need a break – You will get tired. You will need some down time to recharge. It is better to ride the wave when you are strong and can maintain your focus then to try to fake your way and fall off.

Accepting that nothing is secure – Jobs, relationships, health, money, etc. will always change. Accept that at any time, they can be taken from you. The more you let go of the attachment to them, the freer you will become.

Everything is work – Regardless of what you do, or want to do, it takes effort. Know how to acquire the stamina required for the task at hand. There are no free rides and everything you do requires your power.

Maintain your faith – Never give up on something you want. If you truly want it and are willing to work for it, you will get it. Once you put something in motion and move towards it, things happen. They are called miracles and they happen to you all the time.

The Ultimate Guide to Life Surfing has real-life stories of hardships caused by change. I relate the steps in the "CHARM" process to these stories with exercises and techniques aimed to show how Life Surfing is a way of coping with hardship and living a more balanced life.

Yes, there is hope! Whether you want to begin becoming a life surfer or enhance your current Life Surfing skills, you can incorporate these essential skills to give you balance and more self-control.

Now is the time for you to have a check-up from the neck up. Be honest with yourself when you answer these questions:

Do you want to have more control of your life?

Do you want the courage and confidence to try new things in your life?

Do you want to remain calm and focused when hit with unexpected news?

Do you want to maintain your energy and stamina amid your hectic lifestyle?

Do you want to move beyond the sadness caused by hardships?

Do you want to stop thinking you can't and start believing you can?

I'm sure you said yes to more than one of these questions. Then it's time to begin learning how to become a life surfer.

"Life is a series of natural and spontaneous changes. Don't resist them - that only creates sorrow. Let reality be reality. Let things flow naturally forward in whatever way they like." Lao-Tse

2. RIDE THE WAVE

Daniel's wave hit about two years ago. He never saw it coming. He worked at his job as a computer analyst for seven years and was considered a star performer. He was promoted twice and found himself on the fast track to the top. He earned a handsome salary, had been married for nine years, and had two children and a very nice home.

Daniels's life was, or at least he believed was, secure. He had everything he could want: a great job, a wonderful wife, two lovely children, and a magnificent home. He was on top of the world and felt invincible. He was living the life he dreamed about.

Then one day, it all changed. Daniel was called into his boss's office late one Friday afternoon and told that, due to downsizing, he was being laid off and should not to report back to work on Monday. He would be paid through the end of the month and was instructed to clean out his desk and take home his personal belongings. He was asked not to discuss this with his fellow employees and was unemployed by the end of that workday.

In that moment, Daniel's life dramatically changed. Unknown to him at the time, nothing would remain the same for him. That initial wave, in a ripple effect, generated additional waves. Since that fateful afternoon, he has not been able to find a similar job. He searched for a job for over eighteen months. He finally found one and earns much less than what he used to. His wife left him and took their children with her. He had to sell his house and now lives in a one-bedroom apartment. He is miserable and refers to his life as a waste. He sees himself as bleeding and doesn't know how to make it stop. Life just seems to be getting worse, and his willingness to fight and remain positive has diminished greatly. He doesn't know what to do to make things better, and is desperate for something good to come his way.

This is a sad story, and my heart goes out to Daniel. As you read this story, it may relate to a similar event in your life, or someone else's you know. In any case, it demonstrates the stress and anxieties we all feel associated with our turbulent times. Businesses are faced with doing more with less and have to make the tough decisions of letting good people go. Some of us, like Daniel, get caught in that crossfire and experience tragic, horrific events that cause us to bleed. To make matters worse, whatever we try to do can't seem to make it stop.

Not only has life become more challenging for Daniel, but it has also become much more challenging for those who remain with his employer. Imagine if you worked with Daniel in his department and you were among the few still employed.

This now creates a whole new set of stress for you. Someone has to take up the slack for Daniel's workload, and that is usually dumped on those left. Tag, you're it. You have now been told that you will absorb the brunt of Daniel's workload. Your performance expectations will not change, and if you want to keep your job, you'll not complain and just do the work. You are now joining the ranks of getting more work done with fewer resources. It seems to be the norm in today's organizations.

None of us wants it this way, but what can we do about it? We can't control the economy or generate more jobs. We can't force people to love us and not leave us. We don't determine who lives or dies and when. We can't always pick what changes we want and when they will happen. Life has become a roller coaster ride with twists and turns that are way beyond our control.

In today's world, the unfortunate fact is that our lives are complicated. Regardless of our employment status, we seem to have more things to accomplish while feeling as if we have less time and resources to complete them. We feel more pressure than ever before and can't get room to breathe. The truth is, we have resolved ourselves to this new lifestyle and are trying to be content with it. We all feel, at times, overwhelmed in some way. It is becoming more and more difficult to create a work/life balance. Learning Life Surfing skills will help us find this balance and give us the self-confidence and self-control we need to maintain our equilibrium.

First, you must acknowledge that, regardless of how people or events influence your life, you and only you have the ability to do anything about your life. Whether at the current time you like yourself and your life or not, there are things you may want to change. It could be the way you look or feel. It could be finding a way to enhance your career or position in life. How about creating more successful relationships? Whatever the case, this book can help. Why *this* book?

Because you can immediately begin to use these hands-on practical techniques to teach you how to life surf. They have proven to be successful for people from various backgrounds living in different environments. The techniques are universal and will work for you. The only stipulation is that you make the effort and try them. Read on and you will learn how to life surf and be in better control of your life amid changes. You will learn how to make the adjustments you want, in the way you want.

A difficult challenge most of us will face is that life is not always the way we want it to be. In some ways, modern technology has made our lives easier; in other ways, it has made life more complicated. It's interesting that futurists predicted fifty years ago that by the year 2000, we would be working a twenty-hour week and would not know what to do with our free time.

Now a few years into a new millennium, for most of us this is certainly not the case. Instead of working twenty hours a week, many of us find ourselves working fifty to sixty. Due to economics, many organizations have had to reduce their staffs though downsizing and layoffs. Still, the same work is expected to be done and our workday is so full trying to meet that demand that many of us take our work home to catch up. I know many managers who do not have the time to read and reply to their e-mail because their days are spent putting out fires. With the advent of e-mail, cellular phones, portable computers, and pocket PCs, we can now work anywhere and anytime. And all too often, we <u>must</u> work anywhere...and at any time.

So how do we handle the complications of life? Certainly our schools haven't prepared us to deal with life's uncertainties. Instead, it is expected that somehow we learn this on our own. Some of us had role models to learn from, while others struggle to figure it out through their own trials and tribulations.

Although most of us receive our formal education in our younger years, life continues to provide learning opportunities through experiences and relationships that teach us lessons along the way. How we respond to these lessons can determine whether we pass or fail in the school of life. The truth is, we never really leave school.

Here is a puzzle exercise for you to try. Even if you have done this before, do it again. Take a pen or pencil, and then look at this series of nine dots. Without lifting your pen or pencil or going back over a line you have drawn, connect all nine dots using only four lines. The solution to this puzzle is on the following page. Don't look at the solution until you give yourself a few minutes to solve it.

```
    o        o        o


    o        o        o


    o        o        o
```

When you looked at the puzzle, did you look at the nine dots and see a box? Did you try connecting the dots by staying within the box? If so, you are in the majority.

Our minds are incredibly powerful, yet at times we limit ourselves. We restrict ourselves from using the full capacity of our minds and limit ourselves and react to what is familiar. The diagram of the nine dots looks like a box and this is why we see a box and try to solve the puzzle by drawing lines that stay within the confines of that box.

In order to solve this puzzle and connect all the dots with only four lines you have to go beyond/outside them to do it. Here is what the solution looks like.

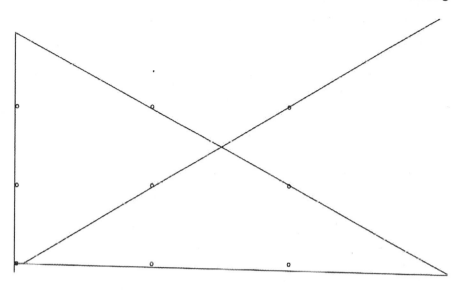

Now I know that some of you have done this exercise before and knew the right answer. It was not new to you. However, let me take this a step further. Look at the diagram below and see the puzzle in a new light.

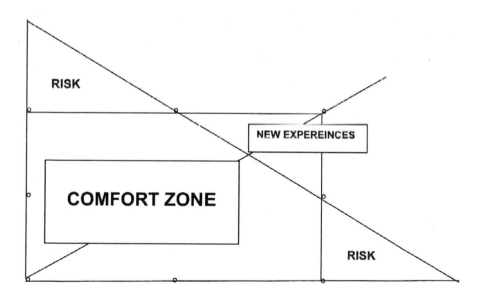

The diagram represents the way we live our lives. The large area inside the box represents the things we have experienced in our lives that are now second-nature; it constitutes the largest part of the diagram. It represents the part of our lives that contains everything that is familiar and offers us little stress. These experiences fall within an area known as our comfort zone. They do not require as much effort and doing them has become part of our everyday/common thinking routine. The experiences require minimal risk because we do them with a high level of competency.

The box in the upper right part of the diagram represents the part of our lives where we try learning something new. These are the experiences we still find challenging. It is the smallest part of the diagram. This area represents those things we avoid because we feel awkward and uncomfortable doing them, like learning a new skill or facing a new experience. When we become adept at this skill, it is moved into the larger area to become part of our comfort zone. These experiences require a medium level of risk because we have a limited competency to do them.

The two areas outside the box represent the unknown and uncharted areas in our lives. These parts of the diagram are the second largest and represent experiences that offer too much risk for us to take. We might know these experiences exist, but will do whatever we can to avoid facing or confronting them. These experiences might be choosing to face the uncertainty of leaving a secure job to travel the world, wrestling an alligator, or finding the courage to leave a relationship in which we are truly unhappy.

They require high risk because although we may have competence, we have a very low level of confidence to tackle them. We create the fear about trying them because we perceive a risk of failure. These experiences scare us into intimidation because no one wants to fail, to be embarrassed, to create pain for themselves, or be eaten by an alligator. Our perception at the outcomes can dictate our actions.

Because of this, it's amazing that most of us would rather remain miserable within our comfort zone than attempt to break out. We reach a level of comfort with what we know and can do, and settle for this. The fear of what may happen if we go outside our comfort zone is so overwhelming that we rationalize excuses in order to avoid these experiences. Some of us do not like the feeling of being out of control, while others do not want to jeopardize what we already have in our possession. The unknown holds a paralyzing fear over us and we can't or won't move!

In some areas of our lives, we become complacent and tolerate where we are, what we have, or what we don't have. We may sink into mediocrity, hoping and wishing for something better to come along. We may blame others and avoid taking responsibility for the way things are. But no matter how hard we try to avoid certain experiences, they continue to pop up over and over again. Bottom line is, you can run but you cannot hide!

As much as I'd like to deny that we confidently face every experience that comes our way, I can't. Instead, I see facing these challenging experiences as opportunities for us to grow and build our character.

Ever ask yourself why you always seem to draw the same types of people into your primary relationships, why you can never advance in your career no matter how hard you work, or why you can never lose weight no matter how hard you try? As long as we remain in our comfort zones, we will continue to ask these questions.

We don't always have choices when forced to learn a new skill or experience a new situation. Life seems to make these choices for us. Even though we accept that relationships and jobs both will eventually end, we resist learning how to pull ourselves up and go on. Although it is difficult, we continue to call on the skills we have stored in our comfort zone to carry us through. As hard as we try, our results never really change.

The area that offers us the greatest opportunities to change our results is when we stretch ourselves to reach beyond our comfort zone and take risks. Although we can still utilize skills we have stored in our comfort zone, we are moving into uncharted territory. We may not have a road map to follow, and all the advice and guidance we received in the past will not make it any easier. The journey can be frightening and intimidating.

I relate the phenomenon of change to the waves in the ocean. The waves can be so beautiful to watch one wave after another reaching the shore. Although perpetual, each wave is different from the next. At times, the waves are very tranquil, and at other times, punishing. Waves are controlled by the differences between high, low, ebb, and neap tides. One thing is certain — regardless of the type of tide, the waves keep coming.

During a hurricane, damaging winds and waves can destroy buildings and homes. Nothing can stop the devastating force. The winds and rage of a hurricane overpower anything we use to prevent its damage. Although what is rebuilt will not be the same, we want it to be better than what it was.

Devastating change often turns to a major disaster when concurrent multiple changes ripple through our lives. An example of this is what occurred on September 11, 2001. The tragedy of that day had tremendous personal impact on our lives, as well as the complete destruction of the World Trade Center buildings. Their crumbling to the ground, which killed thousands of innocent people, generated a ripple effect of change which created war, which affected our economy, which affected the stock market, and which has since affected the job market. Many people developed anxiety disorders because the threat of terrorism continues. It has changed the way we will look at our national security forever. Devastating change in our personal lives, as with Daniel's story, also creates a ripple effect.

As an example, Alice is thirty-seven and a wonderful person. She is very beautiful, kind, and intelligent, with a great sense of humor. She has a good job, a loving husband, and two children. Many envied her and her good life. When Alice was thirty-two, she began to feel unwell. She was unsure what was wrong, as she had always been healthy. She rarely went to a doctor. She continued to feel different for about two months, and then finally went to her doctor. He ran some tests. The results boded ill. He told Alice she had multiple sclerosis. Her life would never be the same. She could not undo the damage to her health, and would have to take medication the rest of her life. There was also a good chance that the illness would continue to worsen and could endanger her life.

Her lifestyle would never be the same. She would have to give up some of the things she loved to do, and face limitations. Suddenly, those who had envied her began to pity her. "What a shame!" they all said. "How could this happen to such a wonderful person?" As with most of us, Alice's health was the most important thing in her life. It can be devastating when we get ill. When you have your health, you have everything!

In life, situations happen that will change us forever. Not all situations are bad, and some can be wonderful. What is true is that the waves of change bring times of jubilation, of tranquility, of uncertainty, as well as devastation. In any case, we may be powerless to stop them. What we can do is learn how to become a life surfer and learn how to ride the waves of change, instead of trying to control the force or direction of them. Like surfers, we can learn to control our balance so we ride the waves of change and don't fall off our board.

How we life surf and ride the wave of change and how we cope after the wave hits is personal. We are all different, and what may work for one might not work for another. Traditional methods taught for coping with change are to eat well, exercise, and relax. That's great as long as you have the discipline and desire to follow that perception. What if you don't? How long will you stay on an exercise program if you don't like to exercise? How long will you stay on a diet if you love chocolate and continue to eat it?

In today's world, there is one true certainty: change, like waves upon the shoreline, will continue to batter us. You will see it both personally and professionally. I encourage you to become a life surfer and learn how to incorporate into your life the techniques within this book. These techniques will become instrumental towards your quest for gaining self-control and self-confidence while surfing life's changes.

So if you are ready, grab your board and let's begin learning the art of Life Surfing.

KEY POINTS FOR LIFE SURFING

At certain points in your life, waves of change will blindside you and produce circumstances that are devastating. In most cases, though, you are always riding the waves, trying to do your best while juggling your priorities. Both take courage to face the unknown. Life Surfers push themselves beyond their comfort zones and face the uncertainty life offers, using their skills to maintain balance.

- No wave of change is the same. Even the low ones can give you trouble. Don't take the small ones for granted.

13

- It's not the board that makes the surfer, but how it is used.

- If you are not willing to challenge yourself and risk a wipe out then don't even bother paddling out.

- "Heaven and Earth are not Humane" – Lao Tzu

"Self-actualization is hard work that involves a calling to service from the external, day-to-day world, not only a yearning from within." Abraham Maslow

3. SAFETY FIRST

The study of psychology and human nature is complicated. I have always tried to glean from my studies what I can practically apply and use in my life. Humanistic psychology has resonated with me from the moment I first read about it because it deals with the world of possibilities and is inspired by people taking positive action for what they believe in. It encourages us to use our minds to choose, to grow, and to create what matters in our lives and world. It helps explain the reasons why we do what we do by looking at our behavior.

Humanistic psychology is not about psychosis or mental instability. It is a natural, healthy way of looking at our behavior. If we can understand our behavior patterns and the reasons we behave the way we do, then it is possible to change our lives by changing our behavior. By putting an emphasis on our consciousness and our human dignity, we have the capability to direct our own destiny.

Abraham Maslow was a humanist. He played a key role in the development of modern humanistic psychology. He is best known for his theory, The Hierarchy of Needs, which is differing levels of motivation that describe the process by which we satisfy our needs and fulfill our potential.

Maslow believed that being forced to live with less than what we want is what creates our depression, despair, alienation, and degree of cynicism. The theory is based on a succession of needs all interrelating to each other. The goal is to satisfy each level of need, thus attaining the ability to reach self-actualization. I see self-actualization as the point where we can reach our potential and perform at high levels without any doubts, ambivalence, or anxiety.

Here is an illustration of Maslow's model:

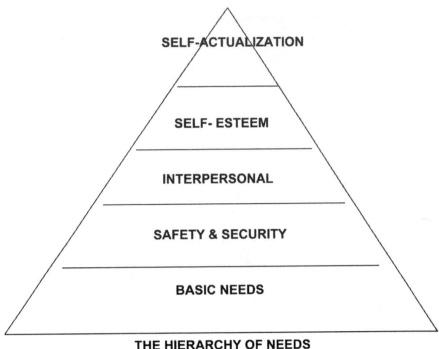

THE HIERARCHY OF NEEDS

The bottom level of the triangle represents our basic needs. These include food, water, and air. Without these, we cannot live.

The next level is safety and security. This includes a place for us to live, money to survive, and a sense of structure and order in our lives.

The third level is interpersonal relationships. This is our ability to relate to others, have meaningful relationships, and experience love and intimacy.

The fourth level is self-esteem, our search for competency, acknowledgement from others, and our self-worth.

The final level is self-actualization or the ability to reach our potential and perform at our highest levels.

Maslow's theory is known throughout the world and accepted in many schools of thought. Allow me to apply Maslow's theory to our ability to ride the wave of change.

Think of a time when you had to do something you were afraid of or intimidated to do. For an example, did you know that the number one fear among Americans is public speaking? Many of us feel very uncomfortable speaking before a group of people. If it helps, you can use this example or another from your personal experience for this illustration.

You are in an audience of 500 people attending a lecture. The presenter singles you out and asks you to come to the stage and talk to the group for ten minutes. You are not prepared and don't know what to say or where to begin. Before you get out of your chair, you begin to sweat, find it difficult to breathe, and your mouth becomes dry. You begin to breathe quickly and you need something to drink. You are feeling these symptoms because your first level of the hierarchy, basic need, has just become unsteady and has been rocked.

So you take a deep breath, muster your nerve, and begin to rise. Your knees quiver and you hear yourself think, "What am I doing? I can't do this. Who am I kidding? This will be a disaster." Can you relate to this? Remember being there? When you experience these symptoms, your need for safety and security becomes unstable and has been rocked.

As you walk to the stage, you hear people whispering. You feel very self-conscious. You know they are talking about you. You think they are probably trying to figure out who you are. Maybe they are criticizing what you are wearing. You begin to doubt why you ever got up in the first place and begin to develop a sense of distance between you and the audience. The closer you get to the stage, the more self-conscious you become. This triggers you to sweat more profusely, shake more visibly, and breathe even faster. At this point, your need for interpersonal relationships are affected because the reaction from the audience has made you nervous.

While all of this is going on in a matter of minutes, imagine what it is doing to your self-esteem. Do you think you feel very confident at this point? Not really! You are full of self-doubt, becoming more nervous by the second, and want to be anywhere but walking to the stage. You finally get up there, stand behind the podium, look out at the audience, and are gripped with fear. Your stomach is turning upside down, your heart is beating out of control, you continue to sweat, and you open your mouth to speak. Nothing comes out and your heart sinks. You have now experienced your self-esteem being rocked.

Needless to say, how can you expect to perform at your best and reach self-actualization while all this is going on? As you can see, once one level is rocked, it leads directly to the level above it and so on. Regardless of which level is unsteady, you cannot succeed in reaching high performance when your needs are not being met.

Here is another example occurring in today's corporations that may hit closer to home.

Ted has worked for his company for nine years. He is a good employee and known for doing a good job. He is dependable and a model of integrity. He is a project manager with five direct reports. While working on a project in his office, he receives an e-mail sent to all employees by the vice president of Human Resources. The e-mail states that due to economic conditions, all departments within the organization will be restructuring within the next six months. Layoffs will be avoided if possible, but there are no guarantees. More news will follow in the next few weeks.

When reading this, Ted's heart begins to beat faster. He reads it once and then re-reads it. Stunned and in disbelief, he takes a deep breath and leans back in his chair. His mouth becomes dry and he can sense himself becoming nervous. He does not know what to do, and at this point does not want to continue working on his project.

His mind is racing a mile a minute and is out of control. His initial thoughts are, "What will happen to me? Will I lose my job? What will this mean to my income? Will this affect my ability to pay for college for my kids? Will I be able to keep the house I bought two years ago?"

As Ted continues to process this news, his questions continue to circulate within his mind. Letting the news sink in a little, he decides to call his friend Mark, another manager in the company.

"Mark," he says, "what do you make of this news?"

"Not sure," replies Mark, "it's a shock to me."

"Me too," says Ted incredulously. "Do you think John (Ted and Mark's boss) knows anything more?"

Mark replies, "I don't know, let's go ask him."

Does any of this sound familiar? Regardless of the specific circumstances, when we are faced with news of this nature, we immediately begin to question how it will affect us personally. This is because unsettling news shakes our need for security and safety. It is a normal and expected response. The scenario above begins to launch an entire set of events. Let's continue the scenario.

Ted and Mark visit their boss and he tells them that he does not know anything more. He knew about this a few days ago, but that is all. Ted and Mark leave John's office questioning whether John has been honest with them. They think he knows more and won't tell.

Upon returning to his office, Ted checks his voice mail and learns that three of his direct reports have left messages for him. When he calls them back, they ask him the same questions he and Mark asked John. Ted tells his direct reports he does not know anything more and that the news came as a shock to him too.

If Ted thinks his boss knows more than he is telling him, then how do you think Ted's direct reports feel? Naturally, they could feel the same way. All of a sudden, there is mistrust within the organization, with employees feeling left out and uninformed. They believe that management knows more but is not telling them, thus rocking their interpersonal relationships.

At this point, do you think Ted and his direct reports are able to produce work at high levels of performance? Definitely not! How high do you think Ted's self-esteem is? How can he feel good about himself with all this going on? In a matter of hours, Ted's life has become tumultuous. Focusing on work and producing quality results are no longer on his list of priorities.

In situations like these, we usually get beyond our basic needs quickly. Unless we breathe, eat, or drink, we die. We have learned basic survival skills and in some cases, under this type of stress, we actually eat and drink more than usual. It is not as easy as we move up the hierarchy to the next three levels of needs (interpersonal relationships, self-esteem, and self-actualization).

As long as Ted's need for safety and security are not met, he will continue to be complacent. He will continue to mistrust his management and senior leadership of the organization, and defend himself with his direct reports. Although the demands of his job have not changed, he will continue to find it challenging to stay focused. After this shocking news settles in for a few hours, the rumor mill begins.

This is when pockets of employees begin to ask each other what is going on. If they don't get answers from management, they will begin to surmise and create their own. Pretty soon, there develops a "rumor-of-the-day." Some employees will continue to partake in the rumor mill game, while in time others will become agitated and remove themselves from playing that game.

Regardless of which direction employees go, the fact remains that until management provides accurate information and clear direction, no one will feel safe or trust anyone else.

What's interesting is that eventually Ted will get tired of the rumor mill and find ways to rise above it. He will see the rumors as distractions and avoid them. He will ignore what others say and try to focus on the work he needs to do or find something else to keep him occupied. Until Ted knows the truth of the matter, he has resigned himself to do his job and not speculate.

Even though he has conquered the rumor mill game at work, the topic follows him wherever he goes. His wife and family continue to ask him how things are going at work. Has he heard any news? Will he keep his job? It's the topic of discussion every time they get together for a family occasion. It's easier for Ted to have his need for safety and security met at work because he can tell his co-workers to leave him alone. It's not so easy with his family.

In the mid -1950s, Abraham Maslow began to write books that focused on management theory. He said that work should be an extension of our personality and provide the opportunity for us to challenge ourselves. He also said that we should be passionate towards the work we do. If we are not challenged and don't have the opportunity to reach our potential in our current job, then we will leave and find one that affords us this opportunity. He also stated that a manager's job is to create an environment for everyone to be successful. To do this, the manager needs to develop the skills of his or her direct reports. Amazingly, his words are just as relevant today than they were fifty years ago.

It was common for the parents of the Baby Boomer generation to work for twenty five years for the same company and retire with a gold watch. There wasn't a lot of change in the workforce and a manager's focus was on managing processes, not people. There was not much dissent among the workforce; as long as you received good pay, you stayed in your job. Upward mobility was scarce and unless a manager retired, there were few management positions available. Managers did not develop employees into future managers, since there were so few positions available. Because of this, managers protected their positions and kept distance from their employees in an effort to keep their own jobs.

Today, change in our lives is happening faster every day. The new business world of globalization, mergers, acquisitions, competition for customer share, and shareholder pressures have created times of uncertainty. Gone are the days of working for one company and retiring with a gold watch. The technical revolution has given birth to more start-up companies and more people opening their own businesses. In today's world, job opportunities are more plentiful, and according to research conducted by business journals, the average person will work for twelve different companies in his or her lifetime. Due to the instability in our business world, there is more dissent among the workforce.

Managers today not only manage processes alone, they have to also balance that with managing people. Absenteeism, tardiness, and performance deficiencies have become the norm. Business is moving so fast that it has created the need for more managers and upward mobility. In many businesses, the belief is that if you do not like your job today, don't fret; it will change in six months.

Maslow believed that as a manager, your role was to find your replacement. If you train others to do the job you are doing, then you will be noticed as a good manager and be promoted. There have been countless times when managers have been overlooked for a promotion because senior management was concerned that if this manager was promoted, there would be no one capable to take his or her place. Maslow's belief of finding your own replacement rested on making others feel safe and secure in the work environment.

Unless Ted, Mark, and the rest of the managers of the company in this scenario fulfill the need of their employees to feel safe, work results will remain inconsistent. Morale will be low and cooperation limited. People will leave the organization and turnover will be high. Hiring replacements will be challenging, since no one wants to work for an organization that is in turmoil. The rumor mill will continue and mistrust will remain high. Ted's life will mirror the atmosphere within the organization. Until he finds a way to rise above the uncertainty and satisfy his need for safety and security, his work will be inconsistent and his life will remain in disarray.

Why is feeling safe and secure so important to our well-being? According to Maslow, it is the second level of the hierarchy, and is the basis for our being productive in life. Let me explain.

The key ingredient in any relationship we have is to feel acknowledged. When we are acknowledged, it tells us we are important to someone and that we have meaning. If we do not experience this, we feel left out. Even strong-willed people with high self-esteem will feel this way. There is no avoiding it. When we feel unacknowledged, we have two choices: (1) feel mistrust and animosity towards the other person, or (2) leave the relationship.

In Ted's case, he and his fellow employees are not being acknowledged by the organization. They do not feel important or wanted. They feel left out and have mistrust for upper management. Some employees will leave because their need for safety and security is too strong. They cannot live with the uncertainly of not knowing if they will have a job when the restructuring occurs. Instead they will leave to find other jobs. For them, any job will do when faced with uncertainty. They will not be as selective, and may settle for jobs they may not really like. Having a steady paycheck satisfies their need for safety and security, and that outweighs being selective. Unfortunately, they rarely stay with one job very long, because as soon as change occurs, they leave. They are usually average workers who will tell you that they can never find the right job. Of course they can't, because until they find a way to feel safe in uncertain environments, they will not find the type of job that will be rewarding for them.

Is this beginning to make sense to you? Can you apply what I have been saying to other areas of your life? Feeling safe and secure relates to more than just our jobs, and affects every area of our lives.

At this point, the question is, how can you feel safe and secure when life throws you for a loop? You know that having others encourage you and push you through the tough times is not enough. All the support in the world will not help if you cannot find ways to feel safe. You can't skip your need for safety and security in the hierarchy and move right to interpersonal relationships or self-esteem. You try to fool those around you by making them believe everything is fine. This can work for a while, but ultimately, the person you need to convince is you.

The journey to self-empowerment, remaining in control, satisfying your needs, and becoming a life surfer so you can successfully ride the wave of change is not as difficult as you may think. If you are ready to take this journey, I ask that you open your mind and heart. The journey begins with you.

KEY POINTS FOR LIFE SURFING

Life surfers assume self-responsibility at all times. They do not get hung up on how bad things have gotten by focusing on the repercussions change brings, but on what they can do about it. They move quickly from thinking what the changes will do to them, to how they can make the most of the situation and become more opportunistic. If life surfers are not in a position to change what is going on outside of them, they put their attention on what is going on inside of them. They do not put themselves at risk unless they are prepared.

- You might be able to see the waves, but not the undertow.

- If you don't know how to surf, take lessons first.

- When the water's cold, wear a wetsuit.

- "Every now and then, go away and have a little relaxation, for when you come back to your work, your judgment will be sure; since to remain constantly at work will cause you to lose power of judgment. Go some distance away because the work appears smaller and more if it can be taken in at a glance, and lack of harmony or proportion is more readily seen." – Leonardo Da Vinci

"Dwell not on the past. Use it to illustrate a point, then leave it behind. Nothing really matters except what you do now in this instant of time. From this moment onward you can be an entirely different person, filled with love and understanding, ready with an outstretched hand, uplifted and positive in every thought and deed."
Eileen Caddy, God Spoke to Me

4. THE ILLUSION OF FEAR

We all have a strong need for control. When we are in control, we feel safe. This need can be met by controlling or at least anticipating the future. We set specific expectations based on what can be controlled or anticipated. We feel in control when the perceived reality matches our expectations. When the perceived reality does not match our expectations, we feel out of control. The feeling of loss of control triggers our need for safety and security, and thus begins our downward spiral.

We feel safe and in control when we get what we want or when we are prepared for what we are not going to get. Our feeling of safety creates within us a sense of balance which helps us remain poised during adversity. When this balance is disrupted, our need for safety and security creates a feeling of uncertainty. In response, we try to adapt to restore balance and our sense of control. If we are successful, our environment once again becomes predictable. Being in a predictable environment makes us feel safe because we are in control.

My rhetorical questions are, What is it we control? Do we control our environment? Do we control what lies outside of us? If we had more control of these, would we still have such a strong need to feel safe and secure?

The secret to gaining control is to not try and control what we can't, but control what we can. We cannot control our significant others. We cannot control our bosses. We cannot control the turbulence betweens nations that causes conflict in our world. The more effort we put into trying to control these outside forces, the more insecure and unsafe we will feel. Instead, focus on what you can control: yourself and how you think, feel, and react. What makes this a challenge is one emotion: *fear.*

By definition, fear is an unpleasant, often strong emotion caused by anticipation or awareness of danger. I find the words "anticipation" and "awareness" especially of interest in this context. When we become afraid, what is it we become afraid of? The questions we ask ourselves when we feel unsafe perpetuate our fear. What we fear is the uncertainty of the unknown, the basic concern about what will happen to us.

When life throws us a curve and forces us to face uncertainty, we naturally retreat into insecurity and fear. We begin to make up all kinds of scenarios that may or may not happen to us. We cannot help but think about worst-case scenarios.

It is difficult to change the way we react to uncertainty, because we have behavioral habits or patterns that are unconscious or automatic. We act and react the same way, time after time, when faced with adversity. To learn effective skills for managing self-control, you (and only you) must become accountable for your own growth. You can and will learn techniques in this book to recognize and break free from the old, negative patterns that make your progress towards self-empowerment rocky.

Ever wonder how your patterns got there? Here's a suggestion: As a good parent, you will naturally be protective of your child. If you see your two-year-old reaching to put his or her hand into a pot of boiling water on the stove, you will yell at him or her to stop. You will run to your child and pull his or her hand away. You will tell your child it is bad to do that and not to do it again. Your panic is reflected to your child, who makes an unconscious recording of the event.

What if you look out your window and notice your four-year-old son climbing a tree in your back yard? Panic-stricken, you run out and yell at him to come down. You tell him he will fall and could get hurt.

There are many times when we tell our children to stop doing things that could be harmful. Our job is to be protective. After all, we believe our children do not know better at such a young age.

In fact, they don't. Our minds do not know the difference between right and wrong until we are a few years old. Prior to that, our minds are growing and absorbing all sorts of knowledge. We are adventurous and do not know fear. Life is full of new experiences for us and we playfully embrace them.

When we were children, we heard our parents tell us "no" more than "yes." We did not understand what was happening, only that our parents wanted us to stop. We continued to be told not to do things, and the reflection of these experiences became ingrained in our minds. As our young minds were forming, we began to associate being adventurous and doing something new and risky with imminent danger. Climbing a tree was fun for us as a toddler, but for our parents, it was frightening. We absorbed their fright and our reaction to their fright during those types of experiences and stored them subconsciously in our minds. As adults, we now automatically and unconsciously associate taking risks with danger and getting hurt. As much as we want to face risk and be adventurous, we create behaviors that were formed as patterns long ago that correlate to these beliefs. Today these behaviors manifest in us as adults as self-doubt and fear.

Winston Churchill said that there is nothing to fear but fear itself. This is such a true statement. Fear is the anticipation of what *could* happen to us. Fear is based on the memories we hold from our experiences in our past. We remember past failures and believe that if they happened once, they will happen again.

I remember a time when I had to have a difficult conversation with one of my direct reports. I had found out through reliable sources that she blew up at another employee and said some things that were not very nice. This was hard for me because she was the best employee on my team. She was my favorite and I could always rely on her. She was my high performer and never demonstrated negative behaviors to me, yet I had been told by my peers she was like this. They had problems with her at times, but I found it hard to believe them. They told me she knew what she needed to do to get her job done and at times she either went through or around others to get what she needed. Although I admire this quality, I can only justify it when done with integrity. When I learned about this incident, I called and told her to meet me first thing in the morning at my office.

I was very uncomfortable facing her, and was not sure what I was going to say. I could not understand how she could behave this way when away from my supervision. I did not want the conversation to dampen her spirits and lessen her desire to work so hard. I also did not want to make her upset or, even worse, angry, and was not looking forward to having this difficult conversation.

I wanted the confrontation to be positive and set my expectation that I would be strong and say the right things. My experience with these types of conversations was limited because it was seldom modeled for me growing up. I was new in management and not the confrontational type. I was nervous, with little confidence in my ability to do this, but I knew the conversation had to take place and I had to face the inevitable. The night before, I kept rehearsing in my head what I was going to say to her. As I paced in circles in the privacy of my room, I went so far as to practice in front of a mirror and kept repeating what I was going to say out loud.

The next morning, we met and I began the conversation. Once she began to ask me questions, the words I spent so much time rehearsing came out all wrong. Despite that, the experience was not so bad. It actually went a lot better that I thought it would. Instead of the conversation deteriorating, we reached an understanding and she was able to accept responsibility for her actions.

I spent all that time rehearsing because I felt very nervous and wanted to have a conversation without upsetting her. I set high expectations for myself, yet I had low confidence. I worked myself up getting ready for our conversation and added a lot of stress and anxiety in the process.

I'm not saying that rehearsing is a bad thing; it's just that we need to focus on our preparation instead of dwelling on the results. If we are prepared and open to an outcome, we will reduce stress and anxiety levels. Once we know the outcome, we will then know what we need to do to face the next step. Here is another way to look at fear. It is not new and has been around for a while, but perhaps it will be new to you.

False

Evidence

Appearing

Real

What this is saying is that fear, by itself, is an illusion. We allow fear to have power over us. It minimizes our ability for self-control. The illusion is that we fear something because of memory recall or what someone else tells us will happen. *How can we fear something that has not happened yet?* A key for self-control is to remember that power resides in the present moment. By focusing on the way we think, feel, and react, we empower ourselves to stay in the present. It is more effective to use our memory to learn from our past mistakes and help us prepare for the future, but do not let the anxiety fear brings immobilize us. The past is behind us and the future is not here yet, so what we do control is what is in the present moment. We will maintain better self-control if we focus on the present, have faith in our capabilities, and are willing to risk facing the unknown.

Easier said than done? Not really. It is all a matter of focus. To help understand this, it will be helpful to explore the way our brain and mind work.

By definition, our brain is the portion of the vertebrate central nervous system that constitutes the organ of thought and neural coordination. It includes all the higher nerve centers, receiving stimuli from the sense organs and interpreting and correlating them to formulate the motor impulses. It is made up of neurons and nutritive structures, is enclosed within the skull, and is contiguous with the spinal cord through the foramen magnum. Boy, is that a mouthful!

In essence, our brain is different from our mind. I compare the brain to the hardware of a computer. The mind is the element (or complex of elements) in an individual that feels, perceives, thinks, wills, and especially, reasons. The mind is our organized conscious and unconscious adaptive mental activity that I compare to software within a computer.

Imagine that you are looking at the side of a person's head. Within his head is his brain. It looks like a lima bean. It is smaller at the forehead and larger towards the back of the head. Looking at the brain this way (see Diagram A below) the mind is divided into three parts. Part 1 (closest to our forehead) is our conscious mind. Part 2 (the middle part) is our pre-conscious mind. Part 3 (furthermost from the forehead and closest to the back of the head) is our sub-conscious mind. These parts have different functions and correlate directly with our ability to manage fear and maintain self-control. Note the illustration below.

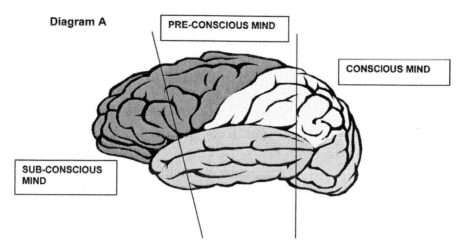

Diagram A

PRE-CONSCIOUS MIND

CONSCIOUS MIND

SUB-CONSCIOUS MIND

Let's examine the roles of the segmented mind. The first part, our conscious mind, only works when we are awake. It deals with the here-and-now and only knows what is happening in the present moment. It governs our ability to focus and maintain a connection with what is happening at any given moment. Hopefully, this is the part of the mind you are using while reading this.

The second part, our pre-conscious mind, works whether we are awake or asleep. It is the part of our mind that stores our memories. Here is where we go to access information from the past. It has the capacity to store unlimited data and the emotions attached to that data. Think of a time when you were getting dressed in the morning to go to work. You were thinking about something you were going to do that day and picturing it in your mind. After you finished thinking about that situation, you began to wonder what you looked like. Did you put on the shirt you wanted to wear? You look in the mirror to see how you look. Did you remember to put on your watch? You check your wrist to be sure. If you were not aware of what you were doing, then who was dressing you? Because getting dressed is an activity you have done thousands of times, it is the work of the pre-conscious mind. The pre-conscious mind can multitask. Since dressing has become second nature, many people do not need to consciously think about dressing when getting dressed. Other examples include thinking about other things while you put on your shoes, walk up the steps in your home, or exercise on a treadmill.

The third part, the sub-conscious mind, works mostly when we are asleep, although it can also function when we are in a relaxed state. This is the part of the mind we can access during meditation. A sudden burst of enlightenment comes from the sub-conscious. How many times have you tossed and turned at night, thinking about a problem, only to awaken with the answer? Think of a time when you were doing something else and all of a sudden, you got the answer to a problem you had been searching for and you said aloud, "I got it!"

Now think of a time when someone asked you a question. You knew the answer, but you forgot it. The harder you tried, the less you remembered. You felt embarrassed because you knew the answer and felt like a fool. You keep trying to remember, but no luck. Eventually you stopped and went on to something else. Ten minutes later, you suddenly remembered.

Here is a story my wife told me that is a great example of this. She and I had only been dating for a few months when she went to dinner with a friend she hadn't seen in a while. During the meal, her friend wanted my then lady friend to tell her all about this new guy she was dating, which she proceeded to do. Her friend then asked what my name was. My future wife drew a blank. She became flustered and could not recall it. Instead of telling her my name, she said to her friend, "You know, what's-his-name. Yea, that's it! What's-his-name!" They went on to continue their meal and discuss other things, when all of a sudden she blurted out, "Norm, his name is Norm!"

My wife still tells this story at parties and we continue to laugh when she tells it. She recalls that she felt like such an idiot because, of course, she did know my name, but for the life of her, could not tell her friend when asked.

Have you ever wondered how this happens? There is an explanation. An amazing thing happens within our mind. Our ability to focus is a component of the conscious part of our mind, and when we focus on something, we use only the conscious part of our mind. We block ourselves from utilizing the pre- and sub-conscious parts of our mind. Since the answer lies in your memory, it is stored in the pre-conscious part of your mind. The harder we try to find the answer, the harder we focus. The harder we focus, the more we only use the conscious part of our mind and thus block ourselves from retrieving our answer. After we stop focusing, we move out of the conscious part of our mind and have access to the pre-conscious again. When this happens, all of a sudden we have our answer.

What's even more interesting is that we already know this on a deeper level. How many times have you hit your forehead with your hand when trying to search for an elusive answer? We know we are trying to access our conscious mind. What we don't know is that we are blocking ourselves from using the pre-conscious to give us the answer. We never see someone hit the back of their head when he or she is trying to search for elusive information.

Understanding this, let's apply it to your ability to manage your anxiety. Remember, anxiety comes from our fears. Our fears come from our past memories. If power is truly in the present moment, then fear lives in the pre-conscious mind as emotions attached to our memories. Fear does not exist in the conscious mind. We remain empowered when we focus using the conscious part of our mind. Once we lose focus and begin to process our thoughts or daydreams, we enter the pre-conscious, where fear can rise and affect us. Staying focused on one thing at a time is the key. To find this key, let's move to the next chapter and do an attitude check.

KEY POINTS FOR LIFE SURFING

Everyone becomes afraid when they feel they have lost control. This is normal. Good life surfers never lose their focus. They know if they do, they may lose their balance and fall. Life surfers minimize their fears by concentrating only on what they can see, hear, smell, touch, or physically feel. If it is not there, it's not real. They only concern themselves with what is real. If it is not real, it's not worth their time to become distracted.

- Just because I wiped out last ride does not mean I will this time.

- Practice every day on the small waves until you know you can tackle the big ones.

- Never lose your concentration, regardless of how easy the ride.

- "Yesterday is but today's memory and tomorrow is today's dream" – Kahil Gibran The Prophet

"Life is the movie you see through your own eyes. It makes no difference what's happening out there. It's how you take it that counts." Dennis Waitley, *The Winner's Edge*

5. RESULTS PROVE INTENTIONS

It happened when I was breaking into my management consultant career. I was hired by the vice president of Human Resources to oversee creating and delivering developmental training courses for an insurance company whose corporate office was located in Philadelphia, Pennsylvania. They had around 3,000 employees in five districts located in Philadelphia, Boston, Baltimore, Richmond, and Charlotte. They wanted me to develop and teach courses focused on communication skills, leadership development, and conflict resolution for everyone except senior management. The courses would be taught in each of the districts to reduce travel for their employees. Each district had a general manager who would support my training efforts within their district.

I had been with the company about five months when enrollment in my courses began to drop. Employees signed up ahead of time, which showed full enrollment to my training administrator during the pre-registration phase, but people were not showing up the day of the class. I let this go on for about a month and then brought it to the attention of the general managers. They did not seem to care and told me to train those who showed up. I spoke to the VP of Human Resources, and she told me that a lot was going on and these employees needed to be doing their jobs the day of the training and would reschedule.

Over the next few months, the no-shows kept increasing. There were times I would teach a course to only five or six people instead of a full class of thirty. People were rescheduling, but still not showing up. I was becoming concerned that this continued trend would diminish the credibility of the courses. The company was paying for my travel expenses and eventually they might decide to eliminate the courses.

Almost one year after I was hired, the company decided to launch a set of three new training courses to infuse new corporate sales and customer service standards (which would be introduced by senior leadership) into the culture of the company. They wanted the courses to be mandatory for every employee, and asked me to create and deliver them. The VP of Human Resources scheduled a meeting with the president of the company, two of the five general managers, and me, to discuss a strategy to launch the training courses.

The president began the meeting by saying that he was looking forward to a successful launch of these courses and the positive impact it would have on the company. Although I had met the president a few times, I did not know him well. After he made his remarks, he looked at me and asked me to discuss my plans to create and deliver these new courses. He wanted a brief outline of the content of the courses and a timetable for their delivery.

I began by telling him that I had concerns about delivering the courses. I was not sure people would show up, even if it was mandatory. I went on to describe what was happening with people not showing up for my courses over the past several months. No one was holding them accountable for showing up, and my class enrollments continued to dwindle. I told him that this was a waste of the company's money and that I did not want to see this happen with these new courses.

When I finished, the president looked at the VP of Human Resources and asked her, "What's going on here? I thought this meeting was to discuss how we were going to launch these courses? Where is this other stuff coming from?"

I looked at the VP of Human Resources, and if looks could kill, I would have been dead. She had fire in her eyes and a look of disbelief on her face. She went on to explain that she was working with the general managers on this problem and promised it would not be an issue moving forward.

The president was satisfied with her answer and went on to ask her how we would launch the program. From that point on, I said very little. I was no longer a factor in the meeting. The president and the rest of them agreed on a time schedule plan to deliver the courses and it was handed to me to make it happen. At the end of the meeting, the president told me he was sorry that I was having trouble getting people to show up for my courses, and to let him know if this trend continued. When the meeting was adjourned, the VP of Human Resources asked me to stay.

When we were alone, she let me have it. She could not believe I told the president about the low enrollments. She wanted to know how I could do this to her. She told me I blindsided her and made her look bad to the rest of the group. I told her I never intended to do that to her, but felt it was important to address that issue. She told me that regardless of my intentions, the damage was done and my credibility was now at stake.

That was one of the most humbling and painful days I have ever had in my career. I was devastated and afraid I would be fired. The meeting left the perception to the people in that room that I was disgruntled with how training was going and was not confident that these new courses would be successful. My perception of the meeting was that I was pointing out a problem to them that, when addressed, would ensure the success of the new courses.

Although I was not fired, my relationship with everyone in that meeting was never the same. I had to work much harder than before to reestablish my credibility with them. I created the courses, delivered them over a four-month period, and the project turned out a tremendous success. Even though attendance was mandatory, not everyone attended the courses. Regardless, the new standards had a positive influence on their business, were successfully infused into the company culture, and are still making an impact today. I stayed with them for another year and voluntarily left to pursue other opportunities.

What happened in that meeting was an epiphany that changed the way I looked at behavior. I did not let the outcome upset me for long, and searched to find out what happened and what I could learn. What I discovered was that, regardless of my intentions, I was angry at the lack of support from the VP of Human Resources and the general managers and their failure to do anything about people skipping my courses. My anger was so strong that it surfaced in the way I addressed the issue with the president. Instead of focusing on the purpose of the meeting, I used the meeting as a platform to air my frustration and my belief that the courses would not be successful because attendance would be low.

At the time, it was not my conscious intention to do this. What I learned from that experience is that the results of my behavior proved my true intentions. I have incorporated the lesson learned from that painful day into my life to help me look at the results of my behaviors to identify what I truly believe about things.

Perhaps you have had a similar experience where your intentions were good, yet you created an outcome that was painful for you and others. To help you understand ways to get control of your behavior, I will first help you explore your attitudes. Let me start by defining some terms.

Intentions are little more than what we have in mind to do or bring about in any situation. This suggests our purpose, design, or goal that we choose to accomplish or attain. You've undoubtedly heard the expression, "The road to hell is paved with good intentions." Intentions do not always match results. There are times when we surprise ourselves and exceed our expectations. We intended to reach a lower target but managed to reach a higher one. There are also times when we do not reach our expectations and, in fact, produce results lower than we expected. Like my meeting, these instances can be embarrassing as well as damaging to us and to others.

Our intentions are plans that we devise to attain a goal. We spend time thinking about a plan of action, and have every desire to be successful. We do not consciously create plans that will be unsuccessful, yet sometimes we behave in ways that sabotage ourselves.

To get a better grasp on our intentions, we need to look at what lies beneath them — at what we actually use to create our plans. The root of our intentions lies in our attitudes. Attitudes are the fuel of our intentions. Attitudes identify our true beliefs about ourselves and the world we live in. These beliefs are hidden deep within us and are difficult to discover. If we are to gain control of our lives and make changes that are successful, we first have to be sure that our beliefs support our actions. The way to do this is to first create the right attitudes and then know how to focus using the conscious part of our minds to direct our intentions away from our fears and towards our objectives.

To gain control of our lives, we must first learn to control our attitudes. There are so many things in our lives we have little or no control over, such as the weather, the job market, and our economy. But there is one aspect that we do have the power to control, and that is our attitude. Each and every moment of every day, we decide what our attitude will be concerning ourselves, our families, our jobs, and so on.

I'm sure we can all agree that there are other factors that influence our attitude, such as our past experiences and experiences told to us by those around us. These factors are harbored within the pre-conscious part of our minds. Regardless, no one can make us think or feel anything without our permission. We hold control over the channels of energy that create our attitudes and therefore the results in our lives.

To gain control over our lives and our destiny, we must learn to gain control over our attitude. Before we can do that, we have to ask ourselves what an attitude is and how we gain control of it.

I believe our attitude is what drives our thoughts, feelings, and behaviors, based on the difference between what we expect and our perceptions of a situation. To better understand this definition, let's examine the major components that make up an attitude.

Expectations are what we desire as results for ourselves, for others, and for situations. Expectations determine our level of contentment and the higher we set them, the more challenging it will be for us to feel contented.

Our Perceptions are developed from memories from past experiences and they help us make meaning of current situations. Our perceptions may or may not be an accurate account of what actually happened, but they do create what we think and feel about a situation.

Our *thoughts* formulate an attitude. Once our mind is aroused, we consciously think about a situation. Thoughts define our state of mind. People who are happy are most likely thinking positive thoughts. Conversely, people who are sad or angry are probably thinking negative thoughts.

Feelings keep our thoughts alive. You can't have an attitude without thoughts or feelings. Feelings promote more thoughts and feelings and keep our mind active.

The amount of *energy* we choose to exert in any situation correlates to or how important it is to us. The greater the importance, the more energy we'll use to exhibit our attitude through what we say, the way we say it, our facial expressions, body language, and behaviors. Energy, just like our attitudes, this can be positive, negative, or neutral in nature.

Actions show the way we response to circumstances. We can either react by taking positive, negative or neutral actions. When we take positive actions we say things like "I can..." or "I will..." On the other hand, when we take negative actions we will say things like "I can't ..." or "I won't ..." neutral actions have us saying things like "I don't want to..." or "I don't care..."

We develop our attitudes while maturing from birth to the age seven. The good news is that we all start out with a clean slate of good attitudes; the bad news is that we later learn how to soil them.

So, how does this happen? Basically, we become biased by our environment. We develop our attitudes from our encounters with our parents, guardians, family members, teachers, and friends — who demonstrate their attitudes through their words and actions. By the time we are two years old, we have already observed more than 8,000 hours of life — both positive and negative. Image what this number looks like when we are seven.

Through the years, I have identified three types of people and attitudes. The first are the *viewers* of life. These are people who go through life watching it happen around them. They limit their life experiences because they choose to remain in their comfort zones and "play it safe" to avoid taking risks. They elect to watch and cheer on others doing challenging tasks instead of risking their own failure or making mistakes. Viewers are usually non-committal and maintain a neutral attitude about life. They get someone else to solve problems and see change as frightening and unnecessary. Viewers watch the future come and go without them. They do not try to control their lives and are usually unemotional, tired, content, indifferent, and detached.

The second are *complainers*. These people stay outside the lines of the action taking place. They don't jump in because they see themselves as experts in the game of life and don't have to. They stand on the sidelines complaining that others are doing it the right way. Complainers usually have a negative attitude about life and find fault in everything. They blame others for causing problems and see change as a pain in their side. They see mistakes as failure and take little or no control over their lives and are usually angry, doubtful, frustrated, pessimistic, and hateful.

The third are the *doers* in the game of life. They enthusiastically await challenges and see them as opportunities to learn something new and to grow, both personally and professionally. They are not afraid to take risks or make mistakes as they see them as pathways for improvement. Doers usually have a positive attitude about life and see something good in every situation. They see problems as opportunities to do things differently, and view change as a sign of growth. They elect to maintain control over their lives and are usually happy, confident, satisfied, optimistic, and loving.

How about doing an attitude check for yourself? Begin by honestly answering this question. What do you value the most?

1. The development of your career

2. The development of your family

3. Your personal development

Every time I ask this question during a Change Management seminar the majority of the audience responds by selecting number three, their personal development, as what they value the most. Then I ask them where they spend the majority of their time. Their answer is at work. So I ask them, if they value their personal development above developing their career and they spend the majority of their time at work, then what's their attitude while at work? Is it always positive? Are there times when they would rather be doing something else besides working? The overwhelming response is always yes. If that's the case then does their behavior at work always match their attitude? Do their intentions always match their results?

Does this ring true with you? To be sure let's validate what type of person have you been lately at home with your family, at work with co-workers and customers, or with yourself? How might people around you describe your attitude? Use the grid and place a check mark under the personality type that best describes your attitude in the following categories.

	Viewer	Complainer	Doer
Home			
Work			
Yourself			

You should also ask people close to you fill in the grid as they see you as well. Do not show them your ratings, and give them a blank grid to fill in. It may be helpful to have them do this anonymously. Then collect their grids and compare theirs to yours. This will offer the best indication of your attitudes.

If you do this, will you be surprised? You may or may not be pleased with the results you've been getting from your actions at home, at work, or in your life? You may see that you are a different type for a certain category, and a combination of two of the three types. If you are not getting the results you want then make adjustments to become a better "doer."

As noted a few pages earlier, we communicate attitudes through the words we use, the tone of our voice, and through our body language and facial expressions. The benefits of a positive attitude are reflected by our attaining better jobs or promotions, successfully completing projects, achieving our goals, satisfying our customers, and maintaining successful relationships.

Being passed over for promotions, losing our job, failing to achieve goals, losing customers, and ruining our relationships are indications of a negative attitude.

Missing opportunities, failing to learn new skills, becoming stagnant, failing to develop relationships, and being excluded from activities are reflections of a neutral attitude.

Since you (and only you) control your thoughts, feelings, and attitudes, you can modify the way you think, feel, and act. By changing your attitude toward another person or situation, you can improve your behavior or actions in ways that will help you get what you want out of the situation. The results of your actions will mirror your true intentions. Although this all seems so logical and is at times difficult, we will explore ways to make it easier in the next few chapters.

KEY POINTS FOR LIFE SURFING

Life surfers are constantly performing a "check-up from the neck up." They know they way the think and feel directly affect their performance. Life surfers understand that confidence is everything. They know that unless you think and feel you can, you won't. Although one great ride is exhilarating, it will not matter unless they believe they will do it again, and again and again. . . .

- If you don't believe you can surf, you won't.

- Riding the best wave is not an outcome, it's a journey.

- My attitude is what stands between me and others as well as between me and myself.

- "You are given the gifts of the gods; you create your reality according to your beliefs. Yours is the creative energy that makes your world. There are no limitations to the self except those you believe in." – Jane Roberts, The Nature of Personal Reality

"At any moment I could start being a better person – but which moment should I choose?" – Ashleigh Brilliant

6. PERSONAL EMPOWERMENT

Think of a person in your life whom you consider powerful. What qualities does this person possess that make him or her powerful? Think of people in your life who made you think they were powerful. Now take a few seconds to clear your mind, and for the next minute, see how many words or phrases you can come up with to define power.

Here are some definitions of power that people have shared with me over the years in my training classes. Power is strength. Control. Charisma. Position in life. Money. Awareness. Knowledge. Job title. Authority. Ability. Right. Command. Supremacy. Muscle. Dominance. Force. Potency. Intensity. Vigor. Weight. Brawn. And might.

Although these do define the word "power," they are not power in its true essence. Instead, they are manifestations of its true essence. I know power exists because I can see and feel it in its manifestations.

In its purest sense, power is energy. How do I know this? I know because I am aware of energy through its manifestations. Let me explain what I mean.

What is energy? Can you see it? Feel it? If you know what to look for, listen to, or touch, then you can. To elaborate on this notion, one form of energy is electricity. You cannot see it or feel it in its pure essence. How do we know electricity exists? We know because we see and feel it through its manifestations.

We see electricity when we watch lightning or turn on the lamps in our homes. Now I'm not advocating you try this, but anyone who has ever tried fixing an electrical outlet without turning off the circuit breaker and touched a live wire has felt the power of electricity. Without being aware of these manifestations, we would never know electricity exists. The same is true with power. Until we are aware of its manifestations, we do not know it exists.

Do you think some people are more powerful than others? Probably so. I have never met anyone who didn't. Why do you think this? It is not because they are more talented or stronger than we. It is because they know how to harness their energy. It is a lot like the power created in a turbulent storm. The winds are intensified to the degree they can destroy buildings. Lightning can split a huge tree. Rain can turn to hail and damage cars and homes. Then, in the blink of an eye, the storm passes and everything is calm. It is like the storm never was. If you did not see the damage, you would never know a storm was there.

Of course, I'm not saying we should all become uncontrollable storms of rage and fury, but we can learn to harness the same level of intensity and use it for our benefit and become more powerful.

During times of change, our need for safety and security diminishes our ability to create and/or maintain our energy levels. The reasons are many, but here is an example to illustrate how we do this to ourselves.

Imagine that I have asked you to contribute money and be part of a group of investors. My plan is to use this money to purchase vast acreage in a remote area and develop an entire community. I show you my plan and promise that I can triple your money if you join me.

You agree, and within a few months, I begin developing the land. I build a section of townhouses, apartments, and single homes. I then build a shopping center, several gas stations, places of worship, restaurants, and a municipal building. I build a power station large enough to deliver heat and electricity to the community. It takes two years to build the community, and in that time, people buy homes and townhouses, and sign leases to rent apartments. Three years later, I present you with your investment, which has tripled as promised.

The demand for living space in our community is overwhelming. It is a huge success. I tell you that if you rejoin my group of investors, I once again can triple your investment. You agree and give me some more money.

Now I add on and build more homes, townhouses, and apartments. Due to the increase of population, I have to build more shopping areas, gas stations, and places of worship. In addition, I need to build schools, since there are enough children living in our community to warrant them. I build a large movie theater complex as well as several health clubs, etc. By now you get the picture. Another three years pass and we have grown into a blossoming, thriving community.

I then call a meeting of all the investors. I present each of you with checks showing a very nice return on your investment. However, I begin to explain that we have a problem. Because of all the new additions, our power station is working overtime. It now has to generate more heat and electricity than before. We have two choices. If we do nothing, the power station will burn out and die. If that happens, we will have many unhappy people and be in lots of legal trouble. The other choice is to add on to the power station and make it suitable to handle the load. This will cost some more money, but it's money well worth spending. I ask which choice you all want to make. By a unanimous vote, you all choose to give back some money to build a larger power station.

In that scenario, it did not seem like difficult choice. We were so committed to the project that we had to build on to the power station. Interestingly enough, this scenario is a representation of our lives.

Because power is energy, in reality we are power stations generating energy. At times, we are faced with so much demand that we burn out. How many of you have too much going on in your life? You volunteer for things, or sometimes got volunteered for things, and before you knew it, your life becomes very complicated. It might not take much more to push you over the edge. Imagine how much more difficult it is for you to juggle everything in your life during times of change and uncertainty.

In our lives, the stress and anxiety we cause ourselves by having too much to handle can cause health problems, even death. The ability to build on and become stronger to handle the load is not easy, since we are at a point where we just do not have any more energy to expend. It takes all the energy we have just to stay on top of everything already in our lives. We swear we cannot take on anything else, but before we know it, here comes more work or personal experiences we must handle. What we face is the reality of needing to let go of something in order to survive. We decide that we can't do it all and we will just have to put off working on or dealing with something until a later time. Instead of having only the choice of letting go of something, what if you could learn how to become stronger and gain more energy to face challenges when these times arise?

Have you ever been told that you only have twenty-four hours in a day and what you do with that time determines your success? If that is true, then you should really consider how you use your energy in that time as the true determination of your success. Think of yourself as a power station. When you feel like you are running low on energy, you become tired. Sleeping, eating healthy foods, and taking vitamins and supplements can help restore your strength. The more you take on, the harder it is to remain strong. This will affect your sleeping and eating patterns and make it more challenging to retain your higher energy levels.

So, is there a secret to harnessing your energy and being more powerful? You bet there is!

Common sense and our experiences have shown that we cannot continue to run ourselves down. We've all been told that you can't burn the candle at both ends. It's not fun going through life feeling physically, emotionally, and mentally challenged. The key to self-empowerment is knowing how to focus our energy and how to make sure we have it moving in the areas we want. I will provide exercises in the first step of the "CHARM" process in Chapter 7 to help develop skills to be in control our thoughts, feelings, and actions.

In my experience, I have found two things that cause us to become disempowered. One is trying to control situations we have no control over, and another is people. Controlling situations will be discussed later. For now, let's look at people.

Ever feel like other people are draining you? They are the people who want more from you than you can easily give, and want to push and pull you all over the place. The more you try, the harder it is to do anything to remedy the situation. They just won't go away. They are always asking you questions that seem simple or wanting you to do things they should be doing themselves. When you see them, you want to turn and run.

What about people who continually anger and upset you because they blame things on you, when what happens is not your fault? Whatever you do is never right or enough for them. They are very demanding and expect too much from you.

I had an uncle who was always nasty. When I was a kid, I remember he was always grumpy and never had nice things to say. He was unpleasant to be around, and I was told by my parents to remain quiet around him and not irritate him. It was as though I had to treat him in a special way because he was the way he was. No one in the family stood up to him or argued with him.

After graduation from college, I decided to take some time to work in the family business. As luck would have it, the business had been started by my grandfather, but since his death, it was run by his son, my uncle. My father was a partner and he brought me into the business.

My uncle was still a nasty man. He had no people skills and could not interact with our customers. That was left for my father and me to do. My uncle was in charge of the finances, ordering, and maintenance. My father was in charge of sales and distribution. We had eleven employees who were co-managed by both my uncle and my father. I came into the business as an employee to learn and do a little of everything.

My uncle would usually arrive in the morning in a bad mood. He was always angry at someone or something, and was very verbal about it. He would complain about the traffic, weather, his wife, kids, or conditions in the world. He always blamed someone else and never admitted any fault of his own. Many times, he would upset customers on the phone or in the office. My father or I had to talk to them afterward, to help calm the waters. Unfortunately, due to my uncle's behavior, we lost some valuable customers and business.

My uncle made all the business decisions. No matter what my father said, my uncle did not care. My uncle, not a very good businessman, made some very bad decisions. To make matters worse, when his decisions proved to be wrong, he blamed either my father or me for not doing it right. Even when evidence proved it was him who was wrong, he would never admit it.

He was also a screamer. When he got angry, he would yell at other people to take out his frustrations. Many times, he would charge into my father's office to unleash a tirade at him and then storm out. I remember watching my father stare at my uncle with a look of shock on his face. My father never argued with my uncle, and just said things to calm him down. When I would talk to my father about this, he would not want to open up. He just kept telling me to ignore my uncle and not let him get the best of me. "Easier said than done," I would tell him.

Although my father tried to remain calm and be a good role model for me, I could see he was upset. At times, his look of rejection and dejection was unbearable. He swallowed his pride but lost his power.

He chose to give in to my uncle, knowing it was a no-win situation. He had to work with him and wanted to make the best of it.

I never knew what to do or how to react when my uncle confronted me. I followed my father's advice and stayed quiet while part of me wanted to cry and another part wanted to rip his head off. My father kept urging me to not let him bother me, but he did.

After working at the business for about two years, I started my graduate courses in psychology. In my second semester, I took a course that changed my life. It was on deviant behavior. My professor began talking about the deviant personality style. The longer he talked, the more I knew he was discussing my uncle. I listened intently. I did not have to take notes because I knew the subject all too well personally. Toward the end of class, we were able to ask questions. He called on me and I stood to speak. I told him about my uncle and asked him how to deal with this type of personality. He told me there were techniques we could use that would help us face people without being confrontational. I told the professor I doubted him and explained some of the things my father was doing when confronted by my uncle.

My professor told the class that these techniques were not about being submissive like my father, but were about being more self-directive. He promised that if I used non-confronting techniques, it would change my uncle's behavior to me. I figured I had nothing to lose and listened to the rest of his lecture.

After the class, I called my father to tell him I was not coming back to work, and went home to my apartment. I needed time to process the discussion and create a non-confronting technique. It took awhile, but I came up with what I thought would be a good technique to use on my uncle the next time he confronted me.

That night, I practiced the technique in front of my mirror for about four hours. Although I was apprehensive, I was determined to do something about my uncle's behavior.

The next morning, I talked myself into being ready to face him. To my dismay, nothing happened that day to allow me to use the technique. I did not have to wait long, though. The following day, I was in my office working on a sales order when I could hear him coming up the hall, yelling for me. He was saying something about my messing up yesterday's sales report. I did not have much time to prepare.

I took a second to take a deep breath and rose to meet him. I walked to my door and met him in the hallway. Immediately, he began yelling at me. I held my hands together behind my back and could feel my knees beginning to shake. I stood as tall as I could and looked him squarely in the eye. I did not say a word, but let him continue to yell at me for something I knew I did not do. It seemed like forever, but after probably two minutes, he stopped yelling and asked if I was going to say anything.

"Are you finished yet?" I replied very calmly, still looking him the eye.

"No, I'm not finished yet," he said very loudly and launched into yet another tirade. He then paused and asked again if I had anything to say. I replied in the same non-threatening voice, "I can see you feel that way."

"Feel that way? What does that mean?" he asked. I remained quiet, stood tall, and continued to look him in the eye. His cheeks filled with air and he turned, walked away, and stormed back down the hall, muttering to himself.

I was so proud of myself. I had done it. The technique worked.

From that point onward, my uncle never bothered me again. Oh, he tried to blame things on me and he confronted me, but I kept using the technique. He became frustrated and stopped. Instead of confronting me, he turned up the heat on my father, blaming him instead of me. Then, an ironic thing happened. My father came to me to ask what I was doing to my uncle. He wanted to know what I did to frustrate my uncle in that way.

"Easy," I told him, "just be neutral."

People like my uncle are difficult to deal with. They can drain our energies and make our lives miserable. Remember the power station illustration? Do you want to continue having people deplete your energy and decrease your power?

Why is this technique so effective? As a rule, people like my uncle are socially impaired. They lack social skills and thrive on making others unhappy. They have low self-esteem, and the more they make others feel unhappy, the better they feel. The trick is, as my father told me, not to let them get to you. It is a game with them. The more you give, the more they take. An altercation with them can leave you drained.

If you do not give any energy, you cannot have any taken.

I now call this technique "The Power of Being Neutral."

Have you ever tired to get a four-year-old child to play a game with you? If he or she does not want to play, there is nothing that will get that child to play with you. You can try sweet talk or being assertive, but the child will block your attempts.

This technique works in the same way. When I did not challenge my uncle or let him upset me, I was showing him that I was unwilling to play his game. He became frustrated and left to find someone else to play with. It will work the same for you.

When you remain neutral, you do not expend any energy. That gives you more for something else. In the years I have been teaching this technique, people always ask me what they can say to another person that will keep things neutral. Some things you can say are these:

- "I can understand you feel/think that way."

- "Is there more you want to say?"

- "What exactly makes you think/feel this way?"

- "I see what you are saying."

Take time to practice this technique, because it may seem very unnatural and uncomfortable in the beginning. Be sure you use a calm tone and speak slowly. Try not to let your excitement or timidity come through in your voice. It is better to do this in a standing position, face to face, eye to eye. It is also better in a neutral location like a hallway or meeting area to keep the person from staying in your space. Keep repeating a neutral statement, even if it sounds foolish to you. Remember that you are not trying to have a conversation that makes sense but are trying to defuse the situation by remaining neutral.

KEY POINTS FOR LIFE SURFING

Life surfers respect the waves of change. They do not think that they are better or more powerful than the waves. Instead, they know that unless they harness their strength, maintain their focus, and remain flexible, the wave will beat them. They realize that some waves are best left alone, and they are selective. They know that once riding a wave, they need to surrender to it, but never to themselves.

- The ocean cannot take from you anything more than you give it.

- I can't ride two waves at the same time. I pick one, forget the other, and give it my best.

- "The feeling of having no power over people and events is generally unbearable to us – when we feel helpless we feel miserable. No one wants less power; everyone wants more. In the world today, however, it is dangerous to seem too power hungry, to be overt with your power moves. We have to seem fair and decent. So we need to be subtle – congenial yet cunning, democratic yet devious." – Robert Green, The 48 Laws of Power

"Like attracts like. Whatever the conscious mind thinks and believes the subconscious identically creates." Brian Adams, How to Succeed

7. PRACTICAL METAPHYSICS

Nothing in our lives stands alone. Everything is connected to something else. This is referred to as humanism, and is the theory of the unity of man and heaven that, from its inception, has characterized Chinese philosophy. The concept of the interconnectedness of all things grew out of social change during the conquest of the Shang by the Chou in 1111 BC. Humanism became the way for man to control his own destiny through human virtue, human effort, and moral deeds, and was the origin of the concept of Yin and Yang, the flowing of two opposites into one.

Chuang Tzu (399 – 295 BC) is one of the more mystical figures in Chinese philosophy. He said that nature is in a state of constant flux, is in constant transformation, and is the universal process that connects all things. He poses these seven questions to ponder: Is the sky revolving around? Is the earth remaining still? Are the sun and moon pursuing each other? Who directs this? Is there a mechanical arrangement that keeps them in motion? Do clouds cause rain or does rain cause the clouds? The wind rises from the north, but now moves to the east, then west, and then suddenly upward.

Humanism evolved and moved beyond Chinese philosophy into the practical, logical art of science. Aristotle continued the humanistic philosophy in his writings on metaphysics. It became formalized three centuries after his death by Andronicus of Rhodes.

Traditionally, metaphysics refers to a branch of science that attempts to understand the fundamental nature of all reality, both visible and invisible. It seeks to describe everything, whether divine or human, in basic, simplistic terms.

Metaphysics is a science that has tried to reach beyond basic physics and enter in the world of mind, body, and spirit. Modern metaphysics encompasses two traditionally contrasted areas. One is mysticism, which are experiences of unity with the loving Ultimate, commonly referred to as God. The second is occultism, which is the extension of knowing (extrasensory perception including telepathy, clairvoyance, precognition, and mediumship) as well as the extension of doing (psychokinesis) beyond the recognized fields of human activity.

The New Age Movement of the 1970s and '80s helped to merge these two areas, bringing them to the forefront of our awareness.

Being pragmatic by nature, I wanted to find practical ways to apply humanism in my life. I looked at theoretical metaphysics as providing the insights for gathering this knowledge through rational thinking. My studies developed what I call "Practical Metaphysics," a way to incorporate this knowledge into practical, day-to-day processes I use in my life.

Metaphysics goes beyond the science of physics, and is composed of several universal laws based on scientific fact. How many of you remember the scientific laws you learned in high school that explain motion and gravity? Most of us don't, yet we accept as fact that when we drop a heavy object, it will fall downward, and when we let go of a helium balloon, it will rise into the sky. We do because it works every time. There is no disputing these truths. Thanks to the insights of Sir Isaac Newton, who formulated these principles, we can understand how this occurs.

To refresh your memory, here are the basic laws of motion and gravity:

1. Inertia – A body in motion will tend to stay in motion.

2. Acceleration – The force acting on an object is equal to the object's mass multiplied by its acceleration.

3. Action & Reaction – For every action, there is an equal and opposite reaction.

4. Gravity – The force between two objects is proportional to the product of their masses and inversely proportional to the square of the distance between them.

I present these laws because physics is an accepted science comprised of many laws. In fact, physics has evolved from the works of Max Planck (theory of quanta) and Albert Einstein (laws of relativity) and others into quantum physics.

Metaphysics, like quantum physics, is a branch of physics. It goes beyond classical physics and consists of universal laws that explain how everything is connected in our lives. Understanding metaphysical laws will help you accelerate your ability to become a better life surfer.

The basic law of metaphysics is that everything in our universe is composed of energy. It is the invisible force that holds and connects everything together. Although everything in our universe contains energy, everything is not equal. The distinguishing factor is the vibrational rate of energy within something. Living matter vibrates at a faster and higher rate than inanimate objects. What separates us from a chair is what scientists refer to as our vibrational rate of the energy.

As described earlier, energy is invisible, but we know it exists because we can see and feel it in its manifestations. Here is a demonstration that will allow you to feel a manifestation of your energy. Rub you hands together, palms facing, as fast as you can for thirty seconds. Now stop and hold them together, palms facing, a few inches apart. You can feel the tingle between your palms. Pull them apart and the feeling changes. It is like you are stretching apart elastic material. The further apart they are, the less you feel the tingle; the closer together, the more intensely you will feel it. This is energy.

A second universal law of metaphysics states that we, as living beings, vibrate at different levels of energy at all times. We vibrate at different levels because our thoughts and feelings determine, at any given moment, if our vibrational levels are fast (meaning a high level of energy) or slow (a low level of energy).

When you feel tired and weak, you are mentally and/or physically drained of energy and need time to rest and recharge. To go to the other extreme, you feel full of energy when you are strong, inspired, and motivated. Your energy vibrates at a faster and higher rate when you are strong. Just like the power station, the stronger our energy is, the more we will be able to handle. If we know how to keep our energy high, we will have a better chance of remaining strong during times of change, stress, and anxiety.

A third universal law of metaphysics states that energy is neutral in polarity. As humans, we have the ability to determine whether our energy is positive or negative. Our thoughts and emotions have a direct effect on its polarity. This is important because a fourth metaphysical law states that like energies attract each other. What this means is that we attract people and life experiences to us that resonate to the polarity of our energy.

Did you ever know a "hard-luck" person? These are people who say that if they did not have bad luck, they'd have no luck at all. This is no accident. They are not victims of circumstance. Usually, as you get to know these people, you find that they have negative attitudes and are self-centered, pessimistic, unwilling to help others, and resistant to personal change. They go through their lives complaining and blaming others or situations for their misfortune. This could not be further from the truth. What is happening is that they have developed such a negative attitude that their energy has become negative in polarity. Therefore, they draw negative experiences such as accidents, misfortunes, and heartache into their lives.

The opposite is also true. Those people who have good things happen to them vibrate with positive energy. They are usually optimistic, good-hearted, and willing to reach out and help others. They are more spiritually attuned and their kindness is repaid by attracting good things into their lives.

This may sound good to you, but so what? My concept of Practical Metaphysics takes these universal laws into account to develop practical, hands-on tools that you can begin using today to become more self-empowered to take charge of your life to ride the wave when things get tough and out of your control. These tools have been taught to thousands of people over the last twenty years, in workshops as well as in corporate training sessions. As I have said to everyone attending one of my sessions, "I cannot do this for you. You and only you can do this for yourself. I will provide the tools and help you create the support mechanisms to ensure your success. If you will agree to do the work, you will be pleased with your results."

The process I will teach you is called **CHARM**. It is an acronym that stands for:

Concentrate

Have a plan

Align your energy

Restructure your relationships

Maintain your focus

I will discuss each step in the "CHARM" process in the next five chapters. I provide practical techniques and exercises to use with each step. Some of them involve mental relaxation and may seem new to you. Remember, they are based on universal laws of metaphysics that, just like the laws of physics, have been proven to work. At this point, you face a choice. You can turn back and continue to search for other ways to manage change in your life, or you can open your mind and heart and continue to read this book. If you make the second choice and want to move forward, you are now ready to learn how to become a better life surfer to ride the wave of changes in your life.

KEY POINTS FOR LIFE SURFING

Life surfers adopt the "CHARM" process as a way of life. When riding a wave, they only concentrate on the present moment, allowing them to be open to be flexible and adjust to the direction and force of the wave. They create and follow a plan to work on their performance, to make sure they get better. They make sure their thoughts and feelings are positive, and when they aren't, take steps to get them there. They always maintain their focus, which more importantly ensures that never lose their optimism and confidence.

- Waves are imminent; if you regret not hopping on a good one, let it go, have faith, another will come along.

- When there is a storm, you can bet the waves will be rough to ride.

- High tide brings better waves to ride.

- "A changed thought system can reverse cause-and-effect as we have come to know it. For most of us this is a very difficult concept to accept because of our resistance to relinquishing the predictability of our past belief system and to assuming responsibility for our thoughts, feelings and reactions. Since we always look out, we can perceive attack outside us only when we have first accepted attack as real within." Gerald G. Jampolosky, Love Is Letting Go of Fear

"The shortest way to do many things is to do only one thing at once."
Samuel Smiles

8. CONCENTRATE – Step 1 in the CHARM Process

Think of a time when you had too much to do and not enough time to get it done. You felt overwhelmed. No matter how hard you tried, you could not seem to get out from under all the demands you faced. The longer it went on, the more things got added to your plate. You found it difficult to concentrate on one thing, because there was just too much to do. Whenever you tried to be focused, you could not maintain it. Life became a struggle and was no fun.

Now think of a time when your perception was otherwise. Your workload was still the same, with too much to do and not enough time to get it done. You had more to do with fewer resources to assist you. The difference is that you found a way to make it work. You were in a great groove and everything you did went well. You had everything under control and, no matter how much was added to your plate, you were able to handle it. Your energy was high and you felt great. Your attitude was positive, and you could whistle while you worked. Something in this scenario was decidedly better than in the first.

What you experienced in the second scenario is what athletes call "being in the zone." When you are in the zone, you feel invincible. Your attitude tells others, "Bring it on!" When you are in the zone, your senses peak and you think clearly. Your motivation and performance are both very high. No obstacle is too large for you to handle. Optimism replaces all fears.

I'm sure you can all think of times when you were in your zone. You may not recall what brought you there, since it just seems to happen. When you know you are there, you figure you might as well take full advantage and conquer your world, because this time will not last and you don't know when you will be in it again.

Being in the zone does not have to just happen to you. Athletes need to prepare themselves to reach it as well as to stay in it. The process of reaching and remaining in the zone begins with your ability to maintain your concentration. To elaborate, let's tie in what's already been discussed in earlier chapters.

When you concentrate, you use the front part of your mind. This puts you in the present moment, where there is only the "now." When you focus your concentration, you use the conscious part of your mind and block all fears from the pre-conscious mind. You also utilize the universal law of metaphysics, which states that power is energy. You are empowered when you focus your energy. You do this when you concentrate and focus your thoughts on only one thing at a time. You do not have to realize all this is happening — instead, when you concentrate, you enter the zone and increase your potential to perform.

The merging of these elements explains why we are focused, motivated, and perform better when we are in the zone. Concentration is the key to get us there whenever we choose. Developing mental discipline will enable us to learn to concentrate amid conflict, chaos, and self-doubt. The more we become mentally disciplined, the more we will be able to master the art of concentration.

Here is an exercise that tests your ability to concentrate. To gain the full benefit of this exercise, read the instructions in the following paragraph and try it before you continue reading.

You will need another person to help you who will be willing to do as you ask. Tell him or her to stand face-to-face about a foot or two away from you. Raise both of your arms, palms facing up, so that they are perpendicular to your shoulders. Using your powers of concentration, try to make your arms as stiff as possible. Ask your helper to stand in front of you and place their left hand under your right forearm and their right hand under your left forearm. Now ask them to gently try to push your arms up so they bend at your elbows. Tell them not to make jerking movements that may hurt you. Instead, you want them to apply steady pressure. They want to try to push your arms up and you want to try to keep them from bending. Again, make sure they do not push hard, but apply steady pressure. Now try it before you continue reading.

How did it go? Were you able to keep your arms straight? Try it again, but this time notice what you are thinking and doing to keep them from bending. Did you flex the muscles in your body to help you resist the force? Did you grimace or clench your teeth? Did you make any sounds? Did you find yourself pushing, tensing your arms to resist the force?

If you did, then I ask you: why? What made you do these things? Did I ask you to do them?

You did them because you were drawing on experience from your pre-conscious mind to help you. You knew that, in order to resist the force, you had to be stronger. So you did what you have always done and added more to the exercise than requested. By doing this, did you concentrate? You weren't if you were using the pre-conscious part of your mind.

This time, let's try a new approach. Raise your arms up again, but visualize that your arms have become an iron beam like the ones used in the construction of buildings. Just concentrate and make a mental picture of this iron beam and nothing else. Imagine that your arms are the beam. Take about fifteen seconds to focus on your arms being this iron beam, and when you are concentrating on the beam and only the beam, nod your head. Let your partner know that when you nod your head he or she can begin to push up your forearms.

Notice a difference? You should. This time your partner should not be able to bend your arms up at your elbows. Your arms remain straight with very little resistance on your part. You do not have to dip into your pre-conscious to help you. Your body already knows what is expected. All you have to do is concentrate and let nature take its course.

If you doubt your results, try this exercise with different people. No matter who they are or how many times you try, if you concentrate, the results will be the same. Not only will it be easier when you concentrate, it will be effortless and more fun. No more grimacing, flexing your body, or resisting. No more wasting unneeded energy that can deplete you. Your power station is strong as you exert only the amount of energy required to do this exercise and reserve the rest for something else. You performance is increased and you succeed. Welcome to the zone.

Now you see that it is possible to get there on your own. Learning to concentrate is not easy. It takes work. The best way I have found to develop the art of concentration is to work on mental discipline. Once you have practiced and worked on enhancing your mental discipline, you will control the skill level of your concentration.

To help you do this, I present several mental discipline exercises to practice. Do these regularly and be patient. Results will not happen tomorrow. Remember that you have been doing things the same way for a long time now. It is unconscious behavior for you. In order to change it, you will have to practice these exercises regularly — several times a day for a month or two. Do not give up. They work.

The easiest and least time-consuming exercises can be done all the time. Just be aware of what is going on while you are involved in activities. For example, pay attention to everything around you when you are driving a car. Too many times you get in a car, drive to your destination, and upon arriving, wonder how you got there. You have no recollection of going through intersections, stopping at lights, or seeing the traffic around you. You were in a world far away. If you do not remember how you got to where you were going, then who was driving? Of course it was you, but you were not using the conscious part of your mind. Since driving has become second nature, you relegate the skill to your pre-conscious mind and go on auto pilot. In contrast, when driving was new to you, you paid closer attention to every detail and stayed focused by using the conscious part of your mind.

Every time you drive a car, make sure you pay attention to every detail. Do not let your mind wander. Keep focused on the road, the traffic, the lights, and the scenery. Not only will it make you a safer driver, it will help develop better mental discipline.

Here are a few quick exercises that are good when you begin your effort to increase your powers of concentration.

1. When you go into a room for the first time, shut your eyes and for a second and see how many objects in the room you can identify. Are there tables, chairs, furniture, or pictures? What are the colors of the walls? Do this whenever you enter a new room.

2. Buy a box of stick matches. Dump them on a table. Put them back in the box with the match heads facing the same way. Then dump them again. Now put them back with every third match head facing the other way.

3. In the evening, recall what you ate for breakfast. What did you do when you first left the house after breakfast? What did you first see after leaving the house? What did you do? Spend about three or four minutes on this activity, no more. The next day, recall what you did after lunch. Do this exercise for any three- or four-minute period of your day.

4. Do you have steps in your home? If so, you use them many times during the day. Do you know how many steps there are? When you use them, you are always thinking about something else. From now on, count each step as you use them. Stay in the present and use the conscious mind when you use your steps.

There is a great exercise to use when you lose your composure and need to regain your focus. Perhaps you are doing something and get distracted, or you are ready to give a presentation to a group of fellow employees and you become nervous. To gain your composure and focus, try counting backwards from 100, using every third number. It goes like this: 100, 97, 94, 91, 88, etc. It does not take long and can be done silently. No one has to know you are even doing it. By the time you get down to single digits, you have regained composure and your focus. Try doing this four or five times a day. Once you get the hang of it and it becomes familiar, change it to every fourth number. You can also use letters of the alphabet or other sets of numbers. Start at 555 and count backwards using every third number. This is a great exercise to help you gain focus when you are feeling scattered and disoriented.

A variation of this exercise is to mentally multiply any two-digit number by another two-digit number. An example is to multiply 39 x 47. You cannot use your fingers or pen and paper. You can only use your mind. In the beginning, the numbers will jump around, but with practice, they will stay in place and you will be able to do this. Once you get the hang of this, try using three-digit numbers.

Now here's an exercise that's fun and easy to do. The next time you are seated in an audience, pick someone who is seated five or six rows in front of you. Concentrate on the back of his or her head, and imagine projecting a small beam of light (use a yellow or white color) from your forehead to the back of the person's head. If you concentrate and stay focused on the beam of light, the person will turn around. Don't look surprised, just smile at him or her, and feel good about your efforts. You can try this exercise almost anywhere — while riding on a bus, on an airplane or in a movie theater.

This next exercise is a bit harder and requires more effort. Don't try this right away, but after you have been successful in the previous exercises. Begin by listening to a CD, cassette tape, or record of a piece of classical music. Select one instrument and try to follow that instrument through the entire piece. Block out all the other instruments. Just listen to the one you selected. Keep doing this by selecting another instrument. With practice, you will be able to listen selectively to any instrument you focus on. This will help you become better at selective listening. You will have the mental discipline to focus in on conversations that are important, while also having the ability to block out those that are distracting.

This next exercise is the hardest and is done outdoors. On a day when there are nice big clouds in the sky, I want you to go outside and sit or lie back in the grass. Look up into the sky and pick one cloud. Squint your eyes closed a bit and stare at the middle of the cloud and concentrate on that spot. Maintain your focus and you will begin to see the cloud split exactly where you are focusing. Remain focused for a minute or two. Then look normally and you will see the cloud has split exactly where you were focusing. Not only is this great to enhance your mental discipline, it illustrates another universal law of metaphysics that we will discuss later — energy follows thought

This last exercise is the most challenging and is excellent to use to test your mental discipline abilities. Do not get frustrated if this does not work right away. It takes a lot of patience and practice. Begin by lighting a single candle, and place it on a table about five to six feet from you. Sit in a chair, squint your eyes a bit, and concentrate on the flame. Keep looking at the flame and see it get smaller and smaller. Keep concentrating on it. Once you see the flame become small, keep concentrating until it goes out. Once it does, open your eyes fully to see that the flame is no longer lit.

The exercises I provided will enhance your powers of concentration (the first step in the CHARM process) and help you develop mental discipline. Doing jigsaw puzzles, knitting, needlepoint, and crossword puzzles are all excellent activities for increasing your mental discipline. People who do these types of activities have the ability to block out distractions and remain focused. Your ability to concentrate and have good mental discipline is the first step in becoming a good life surfer. In the next chapter, we'll take a look at step 2 in the CHARM process.

KEY POINTS FOR LIFE SURFING

No matter how difficult or challenging the ride, life surfers always keep their attention on the pulse of the situation. They know exactly what is going on at any given moment. They may not know yet what they will do, but they have a grip on things and focus on assessing what is going on — working towards figuring out their direction. They proactively seek information to make sure they understand the reality of their situation, while constantly doing a personal check to keep themselves balanced.

- You can never stop practicing to become better at Life Surfing.

- Make a mental picture of your ride before you get in the water.

- "Progress is impossible without change, and those who cannot change their minds cannot change anything." George Bernard Shaw

"Go confidently in the direction of your dreams! Live the life you've imagined. As you simplify your life, the laws of the universe will be simpler; solitude will not be solitude, poverty will not be poverty, nor weakness - weakness." Henry David Thoreau

9.   HAVE A PLAN

What happens if you are driving a car and all of a sudden, the steering wheel becomes loose and falls off? You no longer have use of the steering wheel. Where will the car go? In most cases, wherever it wants to. You have lost the ability to control it, so it follows its own path. Given enough time, your car will crash into something, and perhaps cause damage to something or someone.

Now what do you think would happen if I ask you to drive your car from Las Vegas to San Francisco only using first gear? All the other gears have been removed. Think that would be a fun trip for you to take? You'd have to keep your speed to less than twenty miles per hour, so most likely, it wouldn't be that much fun. You would have to drive slowly, and if you tried to go to fast, you'd risk burning out your engine. The trip would take a very long time, and I'm sure it would raise your frustration levels and keep you bored along the way.

What purposes do a steering wheel and gears serve for an automobile? Obviously, we can direct the car with a steering wheel. We navigate turns and curves in the road, avoid damaging potholes in the road, and stay out of the way of other cars on the road.

Having multiple gears allows us to speed up, slow down, and even change direction. By shifting gears, we allow for weather elements, road conditions, and optimize the car's performance. With reverse, we can also back up the car when we need to go in the opposite direction.

A steering wheel and gears, like those in automobiles, are essential to properly operate it. They are just as necessary for our ability to enhance, sustain, and promote our performance. This is step 2 in the CHARM process, and it is about directing and moderating the speed of our efforts to achieve our goals. If we do not have the ability to direct our goals and the paths of our lives, we leave it all up to chance. This is dangerous and usually results in crashes. We never seem to get anywhere or we become upset because we are not where we want to be. Whatever we try to do, we always get the same results. Remember when I spoke about being on a diet? How many diets have you tried without getting the results you want? How much longer will keep trying a different diet expecting better results? Until you steer into a different direction, your results will continue to be the same.

Establishing and maintaining direction is not enough by itself. Shifting gears is what makes it all happen. Knowing when and how to speed up, slow down, and go in reverse are key components. Let's put these skills to work and illustrate how to create successful plans for keeping you empowered amid changes, as well as how to change your behavior patterns. Just the thought of finally losing the weight you have been trying to lose for years is worth the effort.

For years, companies have mastered the ability to get us to use their products by the way they advertise on television. This strategy makes you think of a car, not a horse, when you hear the word "mustang." The ads we see are not about the product as much as what the product will do for our image if we use it. The strategy has made it acceptable for us to grab a beer after work because over the years, 5 P.M. has become known as Miller Time.

Why do we react to ads in the way we do? It's a simple matter of advertising agencies understanding the techniques that alter our behavior. They are the same techniques used by psychologists for behavior modification therapy. These techniques are used by both Alcoholics and Narcotics Anonymous in their Twelve Step programs.

The 12 Steps (also called The 12 Traditions) is a treatment model that has proven itself over time. The focus of the model is spiritual awakening and a relationship with a higher power. The model provides a methodology for recovery as a lifelong spiritual path. Each step leads to the next and continues through one's life as they offer an opportunity to become self-accountable by learning wisdom and compassion. (You will be able to learn more about the Twelve Steps Tradition by reading any Alcoholics or Narcotics Anonymous materials or by doing a search in the web).

The techniques are based on our human response to a stimulus through repetition. When we see or hear the same stimuli over and over again, it automatically becomes part of our sub-conscious mind.

This is why we begin to hum a song we listen to on the radio and don't even like. When we hear this song we don't like enough times, we may eventually even begin to like it. Researchers have found that if we experience the same stimulus repeatedly for seven days in a row, it will become part of our sub-conscious. Once it does, then we unconsciously begin to react to that stimulus.

In my work with clients, I have found that most people who start developing a new habit stop working on it on the fourth day. Then they start again, only to stop again before doing it repeatedly for seven days in a row.

It is challenging to create new or break old habits. We have become so conditioned to the way we do something that it begins to control us. Until we take back control, change will never happen. This is why having a plan is important, but more important is how you work your plan. If you want to lose weight, you have to work on your plan several times a day for seven to fourteen days straight. Although you may say you do this and still do not get results, you have to take it a step further.

The best way to achieve success in making new or breaking old habits is to create a plan that breaks down your goal into simple tasks. A good friend of mine refers to this as "chunking it down." It's like the old question, how do you eat an elephant? The answer is one bite at a time.

It has taken you some time to get where you currently are, so don't expect immediate results. We all want instant gratification, but in order to change our behavior, we must be patient and work on steps to get there. Master the steps and you will achieve your goal.

There are many diets you can try if you want to lose weight. They all encourage you to change what you eat, drink lots of water, and exercise. Because we want instant results, we do it all at the same time. It becomes overwhelming and we revert to old ways. Remember, where you are now is your comfort zone. Getting beyond it involves the risk of the unknown and overcoming your fears and apprehensions. Here is an example of a plan you can use for changing your behavior to lose weight.

Statement of Your Goal	Be very specific. Do not say, "I want to lose weight." What does this mean? What will it look like when you are done? Instead write a goal statement like, "*I will lose 20 pounds by Dec. 1, 2006 (supposing today is June 1, 2006) and manage to keep that weight off for the rest of my life.*"		
ACTION STEPS		**Begin**	**Finish**
1. Drink eight glasses of water a day		June 1	June 15
2. Create a diet journal to track my progress		June 16	June 31
3. Eliminate bread, cake, and pizza from my diet		July 1	July 15
4. Join a health club and begin a workout program		July 16	July 30
5. Eat salad as a meal for either lunch or dinner		Aug. 1	Aug. 15
6. Go to health club at least three times per week		Aug. 16	Aug. 31
7. Keep eliminating sugary foods from my diet		Sept. 1	Sept. 15
8. Eat carrots and celery as snacks between meals		Sept.16	Sept. 31
9. Increase workout plan		Oct. 1	Oct. 15
10. Begin walking on a treadmill three times a week		Oct. 16	Oct. 28
11. Walk at least two miles on a treadmill three times a week		Nov. 1	Nov. 15
12. Buy new clothes to fit my new body		Nov. 16	Nov. 31

This is just an example of a plan. It may not seem realistic for you, but the process works. You can use the template for any goal. Do you want to change your career? Do you want to enhance a relationship?

Are you overwhelmed with too much to do in your life and need a way to make ends meet? Have you been set back by an unexpected health problem and want to begin making the best of it? There are many other questions I could ask, but you need to ask yourself some tough questions to know what type of plan you want to create. You can work on more than one plan at a time, but not more than three.

By creating action steps within each plan, you are forced to focus on one task, and only that task, for a two-week period. By doing this, you will condition yourself to change your behavior and begin doing this task unconsciously. It will become automatic. Then go to the next step. This does not mean you stop doing the first task. You should not have to think about the first task, and that action will become part of your routine. The next step builds onto it, and so forth.

If you focus on one step at a time, you cannot fail. You utilize the concept of empowering yourself through focusing your energy on one task at a time. You chunk the goal down into meaningful but manageable tasks. As you progress from one task to another, you will begin to see results. Remember — do not rush this. If you truly want to make changes that will become more permanent, then take the time to work through your plan.

KEY POINTS FOR LIFE SURFING

Not knowing what to do or what direction to take is fine for life surfers as long as they will be accountable and make it a temporary state. They avoid staying immobile and in self-paralysis. If they make a bad move, they keep moving and work towards a positive result. They try not to take setbacks personally — but accept them as steps in their process towards success.

- Don't analyze things when you start surfing badly. When you are in slump, go surf with the best — let their confidence rub off on you.

- Surfing, like anything else in life, takes planning. Start small and go from there. Be realistic, but plan for greatness.

- "What we are today comes from our thoughts of yesterday, and our present thoughts build our life of tomorrow: Our life is the creation of our mind." The Buddha

- "If you don't know where you're going, you're likely to end up someplace else." Yogi Berra

"Ideas by themselves cannot produce change of being; your effort must go in the right direction, and one must correspond to the other."
P.D.Ouspensky & G.I. Gurdjieff

10. ALIGN YOUR ENERGY

When you open a word processing program like Microsoft Word on your computer, you will notice a blinking line called the cursor on the left side of a blank page. When you hit the enter key on your keyboard, the cursor line moves down one line on the monitor screen. No matter how many times you hit the enter key, it will always move the cursor line down one line on your screen.

Now try a different word processing program. It doesn't matter which one, just that it is different from the one you just opened. For this example, let's say we are using Microsoft Works. You will notice a blank page like before with a blinking cursor line of the left-hand side of the page. Now try the same thing. Hit the enter key on your keyboard. What happens? The cursor line moves down one line on your monitor screen. It is the same stimulus, resulting in the same response.

Amazingly, regardless of how many different word processing software programs you try, you will always get the same response by hitting the enter key on your keyboard. The reason is that all word processing programs are identical. Although some of the commands vary, they are all identical and show you a blinking cursor line on the left-hand side of the page that will move down one line when you hit the enter key on your keyboard.

Let's switch programs. This time, let's open a spreadsheet program like Excel. The first thing you will notice is that there is no longer a blank page. Instead, the page is full of little boxes. Gone is the blinking cursor you saw in the word processing programs. Now when you hit enter, it moves to highlight the box one line below. Regardless of how many times you hit the enter key, it will keep moving down one line to highlight the box located in that space. How does it do this? You are using the same stimulus, hitting the enter key, but you are getting a new response.

Now try opening up a financial software program like Quicken.

When you do, you'll notice how different the monitor screen looks. It's nothing like you saw with word processing or spreadsheets. Now hit the enter key. Nothing happens. How can this be? You are still using the same stimulus, hitting the enter key, but not getting the same response.

Are all software programs created the same? Do they all function in identical ways? The answer is obviously, no! Different types of software programs use different commands and react in different ways when using the keyboard.

So by now, you may be asking yourself, what does this have to do with me? Much more than you think. Think of your brain as your computer. It is the hardware that operates your nervous system and bodily functions, and keeps you alive. Without it, you would not be able to breathe, use your five senses, or have reflex movement.

Now think of your mind as the software installed in your brain. The software is programs which have been stored in your brain over the years. This software is the record of who you are. It houses your memories, likes, dislikes, etc. and is located in the pre-conscious part of your mind. What complicates matters is that your programs are so imbedded, you do not really know what thoughts, feelings, or behaviors are stored in them. We go though our lives, day in and day out, thinking, feeling, and behaving in accordance with what has been stored into these programs.

Because of this, no matter how hard we try, we keep getting the same results from our efforts to make changes in our lives. The problem is not in the way we are trying. The problem is that we have not changed what has been stored into our programs. Until we change what has been stored into our programs, our results will continue to be the same. So without being aware of this, we maintain our stamina and persevere to make changes. Since nothing changes, our frustration builds and we tend to fall back on our old familiar ways. We put blame on outside forces and continue to try to find new ways to make these changes. It is a vicious cycle that never ends. This is why we fall back into our comfort zones so easily. We find it challenging and at times painful enough to make changes in our lives. We do not want to continue to expose ourselves to the frustration and anxiety associated with failed attempts.

So if what has been stored into our programs unconsciously generates our thoughts, feelings, and behaviors towards certain experiences and we don't know what they are, then how do we make changes in our lives? The way is to find the strength to challenge ourselves and persist with designed actions until we break through what has been stored and reprogram it.

It is like going cold turkey to quit smoking. It is very difficult, as the temptation to smoke haunts us, but we continue to be strong and avoid smoking. We use affirmations to confirm our commitment and do whatever it takes to keep from smoking. Some of us create support teams of our friends and family to help deter our temptations; others keep it to themselves and fight the battle alone. Either way, it is difficult to break old habits and create new ones. Whichever way you choose, you are using what is called "singleness of purpose" to help you succeed in your efforts. Without realizing it, you are also using some universal laws of metaphysics too. If you understand these laws, you can make your efforts easier and be more successful in reprogramming the software programs locked deep within your mind.

One of the most powerful laws of metaphysics is "energy follows thought." This is another way of saying that the way we think creates events in our lives. Remember the exercise with the cloud? By focusing on the cloud and concentrating on splitting it in half, you made the cloud split. This exercise demonstrated the metaphysical law by having your thoughts, which are energy, create the outcome of splitting the cloud.

I remember listening to many motivational lectures, either live or on audio tapes, and hearing the speakers talk about the power of our minds. They would talk about how the way we think affects the way we act. Some of these speakers talked about the power of positive thinking. I remember one speaker referring to our self-doubt and fear of changes as "stinking thinking." Another referred to our lack of motivation as "garbage in-garbage out" thinking. The entire premise of self-motivation is the power of positive thinking. I used to smile to myself as I heard them speak, knowing that they were using terms and analogies most of us would accept. In reality, their lectures were based on metaphysical principles most of us could not understand. If these speakers talked about metaphysical laws, it would lessen their credibility. The general public was not ready to accept this fifteen years ago. The time is right to discuss it now.

The power behind positive thinking is aligning your energy to these universal laws of metaphysics. "Energy follows thought" is the metaphysical law behind the power of positive thinking. It is the law that states that the way we think does control the outcome of events in our lives.

It also aligns to another universal law of metaphysics, "Like energies attract like energies." Much like a magnet, the energy we transmit attracts similar energy back to us. If we transmit negative, self-defeating energy, we get back hardship and bad luck. If we transmit positive, self-empowering energy, we get back opportunities for growth and success.

This can be associated with the Pygmalion effect of a self-fulfilling prophecy.

This is a concept taught in basic management training programs in every organization in America. It states that employees are motivated to perform based on what they think will or should happen to them. The expectation is the strength of a person's belief about whether a particular outcome is possible. An employee's first concern is "Can I do it?" Once an employee has performed a task, what happens to them as a result will influence the way they think about their future behavior.

I truly believe we generate the outcome of situations in our lives by the way we think, feel, and behave. Because of this, there are no accidents and no coincidences in life. Everything that happens to us happens for a reason, and is a result of the energy we project. We attract people into our lives for reasons. Some help us as we face adversity, others create new opportunities to learn lessons that help us evolve and become a better human being. Often it takes six months after a traumatic event in our lives before we begin to understand why. If certain things did not happen to us in the way they did, we would not have what we have today. If our lives were stagnant and remained the same, we would become bored. Life is never what we expect because it is full of challenges and hurdles for us to face and overcome in order for us to grow.

Once unexpected change occurs, we have two choices. We can either embrace the change and work towards seizing its opportunities, or deny change and resist it. Whichever choice we make, we must align our energy to support our behavior. To align your energy, you must support your thoughts and feelings with your behavior. It is not necessary to try to figure out your mental programs. You can pretty well know what they are by the results you have received in your past. Most of us have very similar programs, relating back to the formation of our attitudes. Most of us have sub-conscious programs that were created when we were very young that make us believe that taking risks is dangerous. That is why we always go only so far to make changes in our lives rather than go out on a limb and take a huge risk. Once we risk, our mental program kicks in and all our fears with it. This is why personal growth can be so hard. Each time we face a challenge and overcome it, we grow and reprogram one of our mental programs.

It is not difficult to reprogram our software programs. Our medical profession has labeled this process neural plasticity. This is the brain's ability of neural circuitry to acquire, with appropriate training, the capability to adapt and learn to do new things. This essentially means that through conditioning, our mind will rewire itself and replace what has been stored with new data.

The key to changing your programs is to change your thoughts, feelings, and behaviors towards a situation. If it works for programs like The Twelve Step Tradition in Alcoholics and Narcotics Anonymous, then it will work for you too.

The way we believe (what is stored in our programs) creates our attitudes, which are the ways we think and feel. Our attitudes then create our behaviors, which determine the outcome of our life's situations. Here is the formula for why we behave the way we do:

Beliefs create attitudes, which create our thoughts and feelings, which create our behaviors, which determine our results.

If we change our attitudes, we will be able to reprogram our mental programs. In order to change your results, you have to change your behavior. The best way to do this is to commit to a plan of action to change your behavior. The best way to change your behavior is to change what you think and feel. So use the formula in reverse.

Change the way we behave by aligning our thoughts and feelings to a plan of action. This will change our attitude, which will begin to change our beliefs by reprogramming what is stored in our programs.

Once we see results of our new behaviors, we will believe we can reprogram the old program of "I'm afraid to" to "I know I can." Applying the laws of metaphysics will ensure your ability to change behaviors and therefore your results. Remember the progression that everything is energy, energy follows thought, and like energies attract. By combining the first three steps in the CHARM process, you will create a plan of action, and concentrate by focusing your energies to work on each step. As a result, you will begin taking the right steps to alter your attitude, which, in turn, will reprogram your beliefs into new programs that will help you move through the tough times with power and conviction. Once you begin to change the outcome of your life situations in positive ways, you will be ready to move to step 4 in the CHARM process.

KEY POINTS FOR LIFE SURFING

Life surfers know that their thoughts are like boomerangs. They come back to us in manifestations directly related to how they were sent. When they see a wave approaching that will be challenging, instead of launching into it with negative, fearful thoughts, they take a moment to gather their positive thoughts and enter the ride with determination and self-assurance. No matter what happens, they sustain those thoughts. They know that something good will come from their efforts, and once it does, they will be ready to go from there.

- "We are what we think. All that we are arises from our thoughts. With our thoughts we make the world. Speak or act with a pure mind and happiness will follow you as your shadow unshakeable." The Dhammapada

- "Likes attract likes. Whatever the conscious mind thinks and believes the subconscious identically creates." Brian Adams from How To Succeed

- "Until one is committed, there is hesitancy, the chance to draw back, always ineffectiveness concerning all acts of initiative (and creation), there is one elementary truth, the ignorance of which kills countless ideas and splendid plans: that the moment one definitely commits oneself. Then Providence moves too. All sorts of things occur to help one that would never otherwise have occurred. A whole stream of events issues from the decision, raising in one's favour all manner of unforeseen incidents and meetings and material assistance, which no man could have dreamed would have come his way." Anonymous, from the Scottish Himalayan Expedition.

"The most effective way to achieve right relations with any living thing is to look for the best in it, and then help that best into the fullest expression." J. Allen Boone from Kinship with All Life

11.   RESTRUCTURE YOUR RELATIONSHIPS

It's tough enough trying to deal with our own stuff when we are trying to cope with challenging experiences. To complicate matters, our stress is magnified by having to deal with other people's behaviors at the same time. Wouldn't it be great if we had a way to understand people's behavior and strategies that we could use to deal with them that would decrease our stress and make our lives easier?

Think of people who work with you. You can also think about your kids if you are a parent. Now think of a time when someone did something that seemed really foolish to you. You just shook your head in amazement, not believing that this person did that. You could not understand how he or she could do what he or she just did. It made no logical sense to you. Here is an example.

Margaret is a great worker. She has worked for you for four months and you are pleased with her performance. Yesterday afternoon, she left for home two hours before everyone else. She did not tell you in advance, she just left.

You found out about her leaving and it made you angry. "How could she just leave?" you said to yourself. You decided you would talk to her the next morning.

When you saw her the next morning, you asked her to come into your office. You began by reciting the attendance code to her. You told her you were upset and disappointed in her for leaving early. "How could you do that without telling me first?" you asked. You continued to vent your frustration and told her not to let that happen again. This is how you logically saw this situation.

Margaret waits until you finish and addresses your concern. She relates that she is a good employee. She is the only one in your department who stays late to complete her work. She never takes long breaks and never goes out to lunch. She always brings her lunch and eats while she works. She puts in more hours than anyone else in your department. With this in mind, she felt justified about leaving two hours early yesterday. "If this is the way you want it," she says, "then I will not stay late and will leave when everyone else leaves, take the same long breaks as everyone else, and eat my lunch away from my desk, taking the full hour."

Hearing this, you realize that you may now have a larger problem. You do not want to make Margaret complacent and reduce her performance, but at the same time, you need to show the rest of your department that she cannot leave early.

In this example, Margaret's logical rationale is justified as well as yours. Instead of telling her she was wrong and making her feel as if you are attacking her personally, attack the problem not her rationale. Ask yourself what problems are caused by Margaret leaving early. In this case, it was coverage on the phones for your customers.

In times like these, we tend to play amateur psychologist and try to figure out why someone acted in the way he or she did. No matter how hard we try, we cannot make sense of it. As a parent if you ask your kid why he or she did that, his or her response will usually be, "I don't know." As a co-worker, you can ask and will get all sorts of answers that still do not make sense to you.

The more this begins to bother you, the more stress and anxiety you add to your already heavy load. Instead of increasing your stress level, here's how to deal with this.

No matter how foolish or stupid someone else's behavior is to you, it is not to them. People do what they do because at the time of their action, it was logical to them. I am aware of the penalties I can face if I decide to rob a bank. However, if I decide to rob a bank, for whatever reason, it will be because I can justify the motives. It would make perfect sense to me. Your job is not to try and figure out my rationale. Instead, as a supervisor, parent, or friend, you should help me understand why my rationale was not logical for the workplace, your home, etc. You need to help me understand why my behavior caused a problem.

In Margaret's case, you must have her understand why her leaving early was a problem. State only the facts. Explain that because she left early, she was not at her desk to answer the phone. Her absence forced the rest of your team to pick up the slack. You appreciate her efforts and know how hard she works and the sacrifices she makes to do a good job. The problem is that when she is not at her desk, it takes longer for customers' calls to be answered. Her absence hurts your customers, and that hurts the credibility of the department.

By presenting it this way you focus on her behavior, not her rationale. Ask Margaret if she now sees why her leaving early was a problem. Once she agrees, then you can move to the next step, which will be to determine what needs to be done to accommodate her desire to leave early in the future.

Try this with your employees, kids, friends, and family. It will work every time and eliminate some stress and anxiety you do not need.

People's behaviors still fascinate me. I can assign the same task to five people and they will all do it differently. Some will finish it faster than others, some will do only what is required to get the task done, and others will be creative and go beyond what was asked to get the task done. We are all individuals with our own idiosyncrasies. Sometimes these idiosyncrasies drive us nuts. Wouldn't it be great if we knew in advance how people would respond in certain situations? If we knew this, it would certainly help eliminate the stress, frustration, and anxiety we get when dealing with relationships. Here's the good news: you can!

The best techniques for predicting behavior come from the work of Carl Jung. Jung was a Swedish psychologist who is best known for his theory, "The Psychology of Type." Jung spent his life trying to figure out people's behaviors.

He collaborated with Katherine Briggs and her daughter Isabel Myers Briggs to create the Myers-Briggs Type Indicator. This is an assessment tool that is used in many organizations to determine what Jung calls your preferences. There are four preferences and they are:

1. The way we become aware that something exists

2. Decisions we make once we are aware something exists

3. What excites and motivates us

4. The way we behave.

To understand a preference, let's try this short exercise. Go grab a pen and paper. Write your name the way you sign checks. Now do the same thing with the other hand.

Notice that when I asked you to write your name the first time, you did so without thinking. You have done this so many times, it has become automatic. However, when I asked you to do this the second time, there was hesitation. Some of you probably laughed or told yourself it was going to be difficult. Since it is an unfamiliar task, your fears arose and made it more challenging. Now look at the two signatures. Do they look the same? Is the second sloppier? It is almost like learning to write your name in elementary school. The fact is you can write with both hands, but one is better than the other. It is more comfortable since you are so used to using that hand to write your name. It is not that you cannot write with the other hand. You can, but as you see, it is more elementary since you have not developed the skill to write with your other hand.

The same is true with your preferences. You respond the way you do because it is familiar. If you are forced to respond in another way, it creates stress, since it brings up your fears and self-doubt. Jung discovered these preferences are genetic and a part of us since birth. He also found that there are two ways to respond in each preference. These genetic preferences may not have come from your parents, but from other generations. Jung identified these preferences, found that there are two opposite sides to each one, and gave each side a name.

For the sake of learning how to become a good life surfer, I want to discuss just one of the four preferences. This is how we behave. If you understand your preference for the way you behave and the way people using the opposite side of your preference behave, then you can learn how to build rapport. One thing I have learned over the years is to stop waiting for people to change and be more like you. They won't. Instead, learn how to change your behavior to be more like them. You can also use Jung's work to be able to predict how people will react in certain circumstances. Let me illustrate.

They say opposites attract. Jung stated that you will attract the opposite preference for behavior in your primary relationship with your significant other. You do this because what you see in your partner complements what you lack in yourself. This attraction of opposites affords you the opportunity to learn how to do what you are uncomfortable doing, or not have to do it since your partner can. Ideally, this is a perfect partnership; in reality, it can cause stress and conflict. Looking further at these opposites, Jung called one side of the behavior scale the Judging Preference and the other side the Perceiving Preference.

You are one or the other. See if you can identify which one as I describe them.

If you are a Judger, your goal in life is to bring closure to everything you do. You do not like to leave things undone. You have been born with an internal time clock and always seem to be in a hurry. There is never enough time to get things done. You can wake yourself up at a specific time without using an alarm clock and you can tell what time it is, within fifteen minutes, without looking at a clock. You like to arrive at an appointment early and like to get out early. You are always mentally planning ahead and prefer to think through things ahead of time. You want to always be prepared for anything. You will go so far as to prepare plans A, B, and C just to be sure you are ready for anything that might occur.

Because you are such a mental planner, you like to focus on one thing at a time. You can multitask; however, you become absorbed in what you are doing and are intense. You can block out what is going on around you and have good powers of concentration. Your pet peeve in life is being interrupted before you have completed what you are doing. Since you are a pre-planner, you hate when something happens that you have not planned for. Unexpected surprises make you angry and irritable. Once you get a grip on a new surprise, you can regroup and make a new mental plan quickly.

If you are a Perceiver, you are very different. Your mission in life is to offer alternatives to situations and open things up. You are always looking for new ways to do routine tasks. You are not time-conscious and are usually late for appointments. Time is not as important to you because there will always be more time another day. Instead of bringing closure to things, you like to put them off for as long as possible. In fact, you excel at procrastination because you perform better under pressure. You put things off until the last minute to force you into pressure and therefore, into doing better to complete the task.

Procrastination also gives you the opportunity to look at the task and explore new options. Your pet peeve is confinement. You hate being cornered. You do not like working in a small office without any windows. You like large, open spaces with lots of room. You do not like being forced to make a decision until you have had the chance to mull it over for a while. You do not make decisions based on what you want. If you did that, then a Judger would hold you to it, causing confinement because there would be no room for discussion. Instead you make decisions based on what you don't want. That way, there is lots of room for discussion. Let's put these descriptions into real-life situations.

I am a Judger. I am always thinking about what I want to do, when I want to do it, and how to get it done. I am a pre-planner, impatient, and want to get things done so I can move on to something else. Before I knew and applied Jung's Psychology of Type into my life, I used to ask my wife where she wanted to go for dinner. Since opposites attract, of course, she is a Perceiver. Her response was always, "I don't know." To me, a Judger, that is closure. Because she didn't know, I got to make the decision. So I took her to a restaurant I liked.

No sooner had we pulled into the parking lot when she said, "I don't want to go here." I replied, "So where do you want to go?" She would say, "I don't know; anywhere but here." Again that was closure to me and I made another decision. I drove to another restaurant and the same thing happened. By then, I was getting angry. I was upset because she couldn't make up her mind. She could not tell me where to go to eat, but every place I chose was not to her liking. As you can tell, my pre-planned evening out for a nice dinner was turning out to be a nightmare for both of us.

This is typical between couples who are trying to make a decision. It continued to be frustrating for both my wife and me. I used to sit in the car and tell her I would not drive until she picked a place to eat. She did not like this very much, but eventually she picked one. She would say that I was rushing her into make a choice, and if we did not like the restaurant, it was my fault for forcing her to make that decision. Does any of this sound familiar to you? I'm sure it does, as this scenario can apply to many situations in your life.

Now I use a different approach and it works every time. Since I understand that she is a Perceiver and likes to keep things open, I no longer ask her where she wants to go. I ask her where she does not want to go. Remember that Perceivers make decisions based on what they don't want, not on what they want. So now I begin by asking her what she doesn't want to eat. She rules out Chinese and Mexican. I then ask her if Italian or American cuisine works. She thinks a bit and says either is fine. I then ask her if she does not want to go to restaurant A, B, or C. She rules out B, so I confirm that either A or C is good for her. She nods approval and off we go.

After we first married, she asked me to go with her on a Saturday to shop for a new chair for our living room. Being a Judger, I figured that could not take too long, and agreed. What I thought would be a few hours turned into an all-day journey. I kept asking her what she was looking for. Her reply was always, "I'll know when I see it." The longer the day went on, the more irritated I became. I had no way to help her, and felt like a fifth wheel. Finally, at the end of the day, we went back to the first store we visited and bought a chair. I asked her why we had to go all over town when she was able to buy the chair at the first store. She said that she wanted to see what else was out there and then make her decision. I told her if that was the case, then next time, she could go alone and come get me when she was ready to buy. I would gladly go with her to the store of her choice and tell her if I liked her decision. She did not like my suggestion and expressed that if she had to go alone, she did not need me to help at all. The tension was definitely getting thick.

Using Jung's work again has saved me and perhaps my marriage. Now when she asks me to shop for furniture, I take a new approach. I sit her down, use pen and paper, and ask her what she is not looking for. I make a list of everything she does not want. I take the list with us, so that when we arrive at a furniture store, I share this information with the salesperson. Once the salesperson knows this, he or she can direct us to options that I know my wife will like. This strategy has really worked. It cuts our shopping time in half and is a win-win for both my wife and me. I feel more involved in the process and she begins to know more about what she does want by eliminating what she doesn't.

As a Perceiver, my wife does not pre-plan in the way I do. She once came into our family room, saw me watching a ball game on TV in my favorite chair, and said, "Let's go shopping. We need some stuff at the grocery store and I want you to come with me." I responded irritably by saying, "Not now. Can't you see I'm watching a game?"

She walked away. About an hour later, I approached her and told her I was ready to go. She told me that she was angry with me becuase I told her I was not going. I explained that I did not tell her I was not going, I just did not want to go then. It didn't matter; no matter whatever I said, it did not get me out of the doghouse.

Judgers do not like to be surprised. As a Judger, I had my day's activities pre-planned. I mowed the lawn and did my chores so I could have the time to watch the game. She was not aware of this, because I did not tell her. To her, going to the store was no big deal, because all I was doing was watching TV. To me, it was a surprise, because I planned to watch the game and did not want to go then.

Judgers have a tendency to display their displeasure when surprised or interrupted by moaning out loud. Perceivers take this moaning as a personal attack. That could not be further from the truth, because Judgers need to have their hissy fits when an unexpected surprise disrupts their pre-planned schedule. Situations happen like this all the time between Judgers and Perceivers.

Here's a strategy for Perceivers to use with Judgers when interrupting or surprising them. Tell them what you need to say and leave the room. If you stay, you will have to listen to a Judger moaning, and you don't need to hear that. Let the Judger have time for the hissy fit. Once the Judger is done, he or she will reprioritize their schedule and come back to you with options.

Now when my wife comes into the family room and sees me watching a game, she tells me she wants to do something and then leaves the room. When I have had the chance to work it out for myself, I go to her and tell her that I want to finish watching TV and will be ready in an hour. Being a Perceiver, she is much more flexible with her schedule than I, so she is usually fine with that.

Whether you are a Perceiver or Judger, use this strategy when dealing with Judgers. It works every time and will save you stress and anxiety.

There are many other strategies you can use; however, my point is that when you learn to adapt your style to fit others, it lessens your stress and tension and empowers you and your relationships. Jung's work is fascinating and I have listed several books in the bibliography that you can use to further your understanding of The Psychology of Type.

KEY POINTS FOR LIFE SURFING

Just as each wave is different, so are people. Life surfers learn that it increases their stress levels to avoid the people they don't like. They value differences and understand that the potential for growth occurs when there is diversity. Opposing outlooks and opinions can be healthy. Life surfers have leaned to manage abrasive relationships and use their skills to build rapport. They have heard many times that it is easier to attract flies with honey than vinegar.

- Never judge a wave by the way it looks.

- Feel the wave as you ride and become one with it.

- "Of a certainty the man who can see all creatures in himself, himself in all creatures, knows no sorrow." Eesha Upanishad

- "Peace of mind comes from not wanting to change others, but by simply accepting them as they are. True acceptance is always without demands and expectations." Gerald G. Jampolsky from "Love Is Letting Go of Fear"

"Your pain is breaking the shell that encloses your understanding."
Kahil Gibran from The Prophet

12. MAINTAIN YOUR POWER

We have known for hundreds of years that we only use a very small fraction of the total ability of our minds. Brain specialists now know that the average person uses between 5 and 15 percent of the total capability of his or her mind. Think of what we could achieve if we were able to tap into larger percentages of our capacity.

We can develop these innate abilities. Over fifty years ago, John Dickson who was the publisher of the Chicago Tribune , wrote:

> "Life is like a railroad. The vast majority of people are passenger coach and freight cars. They perform a useful service, but cannot make themselves go and have to be pushed or pulled by someone else. Only a few are like the locomotives that move not only themselves, but also countless others. Without them we would have no progress, humanity would stagnate and eventually drift into savagery."

To be empowered, you must become a locomotive. Much has been written about the use of the mind, and that it is our most powerful instrument. Reading is one thing, but learning how to tap into our untapped potential is another. Earlier, I talked about being a power station and having to eliminate or add on to sustain ourselves. We have been discussing reducing stress and anxiety by learning strategies to eliminate unwanted stress. Now let's look at the final step in the "CHARM" process, which offers ways we can build onto our power supply and tap into parts of the mind so that we maintain our power at all times.

When we were born, our physical mind was blank. Thomas Wolfe said, "Naked and alone we come into exile – into the unspeakable and incommunicable prison of this earth." Wofle was describing the fact that we have to learn everything, since everything is new to us. As an infant, we have no skills, no trained brain cells, no thoughts or motion sequences to depend upon. We only have our brain's capacity to direct out primitive reflex actions like crying, smiling, and gurgling. As we develop, we record, retain, and correlate the observations of our senses. Just like programming a computer, we program our minds.

We have already talked about the fact that our thoughts direct our energy and, when focused, are our greatest powers. There are countless events in our history which illustrate how mankind has been altered by new ideas and the thoughts of original thinkers. We cannot deny that thought is powerful and therefore, we can will ourselves to do things we have never done before. The concept of mind over matter is not new. Thoughts can change your life and bring you comfort and wealth or whatever else your desire. Miracles can be accomplished if you master your ability to harness your energy into focused thought.

Do not allow yourself to become discouraged or confused when you try to use your energy of thought and fail to attain your desired results. You may have read or been told by someone to concentrate upon success and visualize yourself enjoying the success you desire. Again, it is easier said than done. The exercises I offered earlier will help you develop your mental discipline that will now enable you to do the exercises I provide in this chapter. These exercises will help you to know how to generate energy through the power of thought. Maintaining your focus to harness this energy is the next step that must be developed if you are to truly become empowered and master your self-control, especially amid chaos.

When life gets out of control, we tend to follow. The exercises I will now offer provide the ability for you to build onto your energy and strengthen yourself when you are mentally distracted, drained, and emotionally distraught. You will become strong when you feel weak and awake when you feel tired. In order to employ these skills, you must learn to tap into this energy, and this requires your will power.

To use the power of thought to its full potential, you must learn to focus your mind without any restrictions from your fears and emotions. The exercises provided on mental discipline are designed to get you to focus your thoughts consciously and with purpose.

Many people take their energy, or the lack of it, for granted. They recognize that others have more or less than they, but rarely give it a thought. It never occurs to them to question why this happens or if there is anything they can do about it. Yet you have the capability to increase your energy at any given time.

In this and in the next few chapters, I will offer exercises that use relaxation and meditation. I know the thought of this may make some of you want to run for the hills. Please do not be afraid or skeptical. Do not associate the exercises with anything that lacks credibility. They are anything but that. In fact, relaxation and meditation are used in many cultures throughout the world. I will not ask you to do anything you do not want to do. Although relaxation and meditation is a form of self-hypnosis, they won't turn you into a chicken. The exercises that follow are designed to give you more self-control and awareness. You will be alert at all times.

Relaxation and meditation are used because they allow us to relax the mind and tap into parts we may have never accessed. I talked briefly about this when I illustrated the three parts of the mind. Meditation and relaxation are the gateway to the sub-conscious part of our mind. When we are awake, our mind is in an alpha state of consciousness. When we use meditation and relaxation, we reach into a beta state of consciousness and that is when we begin to access your sub-conscious (also referred to as your higher) mind.

As an introduction to meditation and relaxation, here is a quick recharging exercise to use when you feel tired or drained and need a quick "pick me up." It is very easy and can be done in only a few minutes.

1. Sit comfortably in a chair with your weight evenly balanced between your feet.

2. Take a deep breath and count to seven. Breathe through your nose and do not count too fast or too slow. Keep your breathing slow and evenly paced.

3. Hold your breath for a count of seven. As you do this, begin to feel your body relax.

4. Exhale through your mouth for a count of seven and imagine that you are releasing all your stress and anxiety as you exhale.

5. Each time you inhale, you breathe in new fresh energy. As you hold your breath, you allow this energy to move through your body, breaking up tension within your body. As you exhale, you let go of the tension.

6. While performing this exercise, keep your jaws closed and clench each hand into a fist. Keep the rest of your body except your jaw and hands relaxed. As you breathe in, focus on the energy moving in from the soles of your feet and up through your body. As you hold your breath, focus on the energy moving throughout your entire body. As you exhale, focus on the energy leaving your body.

7. Perform the inhale, hold, and exhale process seven times.

Now that wasn't so bad, was it? It should make your feel great. In fact it should make you feel so good that within fifteen to twenty minutes, you will feel a surge of energy that will continue for several hours. You will feel invigorated and alive. This exercise can be used as often as you like. I recommend you practice it once a day. It is great to use after lunch to avert that afternoon sleepy period.

Here is an exercise that I like to do in the morning. It goes a step further to involve your ability to visualize.

1. Stand in front of a window or outdoors, facing the sun, erect and relaxed, with your feet touching and arms extended, palms facing up.

2. The sun is our most powerful source of energy. Close your eyes and visualize the sun as this powerful, flaming orb of energy.

3. Mentally focus your thoughts on the sun. Feel its warmth upon your skin.

4. Inhale to a count of five and breathe in the energy of the sun.

5. Hold your breath for a count of five and feel the warmth move through your body.

6. As you slowly exhale, breathe out though your mouth and

imagine your body surrounded by a large yellow ball of energy.

7. Repeat the breathing process ten times.

This exercise is very powerful. You can do this whether the sun is visible or not. Your ability to visualize the sun and feel its energy will be just as effective as if you were standing facing it. Do this in the morning and it will energize you for the entire day.

These two exercises are great to use to recharge your physical energy when you need physical strength. They are also beginning to show you how to relax your mind and reach the alpha stage of consciousness. As you continue to practice these exercises, you will find yourself being able to relax your mind with less effort and in less time. You will eventually reach a point where you will be able to reach a relaxed state in a few seconds by willing yourself. After you reach this point, you can recharge your energy and keep yourself strong at all times. You will not feel as tired during the day, will need less sleep, and stay in better physical, emotional, and mental shape. Now that you know the basics of how you become re-energized, let's move to the next step. This is how to keep your energy strong and positive so you will utilize the universal laws of metaphysics to keep you riding the waves of change with confidence and direction.

KEY POINTS FOR LIFE SURFING

Riding the waves of change can be exhausting. Life surfers find a way to keep going. Sure they need some downtime, but they never let themselves stay down for too long. Life surfers are like the Energizer, they just keep going, and going, and going......

- "Your subconscious mind has the answer. If you are confronted with a problem and you cannot see an immediate answer, assume that your subconscious has the solution and is waiting to reveal it to you.

If an answer does not come, turn the problem over to your subconscious mind. Keep on turning your request over to your subconscious until the answer comes. The response will be a certain feeling of an inner awareness whereby you know what to do. Guidance in all things comes as the still small voice within: It reveals all". – Brian Adams from How to Succeed

- "All the powers of your inner self are set into activation as a result of your conscious beliefs. You have lost a sense of responsibility for your conscious thought because you have been taught that it is what forms your life. You have been told that regardless of your beliefs you are terrorized by your unconscious conditioning. Some of your beliefs originated in your childhood, but you are not at their mercy unless you believe that you are." Jane Roberts from The Nature of Reality

"Men are disturbed not by things that happen, but by their opinion of the things that happen. Epicetus

13. KEEPING YOUR ENERGY POSITIVE WITH HUNA

Max Freedom Long is the author of many books about the psycho-religious system called Huna. Huna (rhymes with the word tuna) is based on Hawaiian methodologies and in Hawaiian means "secret." The origins of Huna can be traced back to the Nile Valley before the building of the Great Pyramid. Practitioners of Huna, called Kahunas, were adept in the control of their psychic abilities, and the folklore of Hawaii is full of the work of the Kahunas.

Kahunas used psychotherapy to treat fixations, psychoses, and complexes. In 1820, a great and wise Kahuna named Hewahewa saw the coming of the Christian missionaries in a vision. Soon after their arrival, the missionaries outlawed all the practices of the Kahuna, and today, they are looked upon with contempt by the pious Christians of Hawaii.

In 1936, after years of study, Max Freedom Long released his first book, *Recovering the Ancient Magic*. That book is now out of print, but since then, he has released many other books on Huna as well as founding Huna Research Associates, a society devoted to the study and development of Huna techniques.

Huna is no longer a secret. There are many books about it and how to apply its techniques. Huna will allow you to understand your personality and how to restructure it. It affords you the opportunity to reclaim your power over your life and become more successful in attaining your goals.

Within Huna is a simple, logical concept. Everything in our universe uses energy or life vitality. This energy or force is used to keep our physical body functioning and for all physical action. The Huna word for this energy is called *mana* (pronounced using long a) which means power. We use mana to think, feel, and act.

There is an energy that connects us to every living being and situation we experience in our lives. This energy is an etheric substance the Kahunas call *aka*. Aka (pronounced aah-kah) has also been called ectoplasm and is a very fluid, sticky, and versatile substance. It can be extended outward in a thread or cord. It clings to all it touches, drawing out a fine thread between itself and that object. We are like a spider in the web of life, connected to all we have ever touched or focused our eyes on. We have woven relationships with situations and people ever since we were born. Our thoughts and emotions flow along these threads of aka substance, providing us with this invisible connection.

These threads, known to Kahunas as aka chords, appear as a gold color when viewed under a red light in a completely dark room. Kirlian photography, which uses an electrical device to record phenomena that are invisible to our physical eyes, has produced pictures of golden light emitting from the body of human beings when they think positive thoughts and feel good, healthy emotions. The same technology captures a dark gray color from human beings when they think negative thoughts and feel harmful, unhealthy emotions.

By working with Huna, we can begin to realize what is holding us back from the life we want to live. Much of this is due to pain inflicted in our past.

We retain a connection to our past not only with our memories, but also within aka chords still connected to the experience. We can often overcome our fears and memories, but still cannot make the changes in our lives we deserve. Until we learn how to disconnect these aka chords, these experiences will continue to hold us back.

Huna allows us to become aware of what we say, think, and do. It interweaves well with the universal laws of metaphysics that state that everything is energy and the energy we project attracts the same back to us.

Regardless of how you think or feel about a person or a situation, you still have aka chord energy connected to it. When you have relationships or situations that are good, the aka chord emanates a bright gold color between you and your relationships and situations. This means that the energy is strong and of a positive nature.

When relationships or situations are no longer loving but become hostile, strained, and oppressive, the aka chord energy mirrors the thoughts and emotions by darkening to a grey color and becomes negative in polarity. The color of the aka energy connected to these relationships and situations does not change, even if you change your thoughts and emotions.

Keeping your energy positive is essential. Remember, we attract what we project. Positive energy will draw back positive experiences, and negative energy will draw back negative experiences. Having a positive attitude and living a loving life will get you two-thirds of the way to being fully empowered to be what you want to be. The last piece is making sure your energy is positive.

Here are two exercises that will ensure this last piece is in place. The first is from Huna and works on aka chords. Kahunas believe our power (called mana in Hawaiian) emanates from our solar plexus. When positive and loving, it is a brilliant gold color. Use this exercise to maintain your positive energy in all your relationships and life situations.

1. Sit comfortably and breathe using the same process described in earlier exercises.

2. Once you are relaxed, focus your concentration on your solar plexus. This is the soft area right below your breast bone. Begin to imagine that with each breath, you take in gold light, and when you exhale, you release it through your solar plexus in a stream of golden light. Imagine that this beam of light surrounds you, encasing you in an orb of golden light.

3. Each time you breathe, breathe in golden light. Each time you exhale, release it through your solar plexus in a beam of light. The more you breathe, the brighter the orb around you becomes.

4. Now think of a person in your life you no longer like, or perhaps someone you have never liked but have to live or work with. Imagine they are standing facing you, about ten feet away. Begin to imagine a chord of light between your solar plexus and theirs. Since this relationship has negative energy attached to it, the chord of light will be dark grey. Underneath the grey is gold, but there is too much negative energy to see it.

5. Place both of your hands around this cord of light as if you were holding onto a rope connecting you to this person. Begin to walk toward them, keeping your hands on the chord. As you walk, you wipe away the negative energy with your hands and turn the grey color to gold. Walk all the way to them until you have cleansed the entire chord and it is completely gold.

6. If you wish to break the relationship with this person, or have already done so physically or emotionally, then use your hands like a scissors and cut the chord. Although you may still see this person in your life, you no longer have any negative energy attached to the relationship.

7. You can do this for as many people or situations as you like.

8. If you want to maintain the relationship to the person or situation, then do not cut the chord, but make sure it shines brightly in gold. Repeat this exercise if the relationship or situation becomes negative again.

This next exercise will keep you empowered when you are in a situation which intimidates or upsets you. Many times, before we realize it, we are in a situation that we are unprepared to handle, a situation that is just downright nasty and intimidates us. Once it is over, we feel so drained, we want to crawl into a hole and die. This exercise will make these reactions go away and keep you empowered when everything else around you is falling apart. The exercise takes some practice, but afterwards can be done instantaneously.

1. Close your eyes and take a deep breath through your nose. Hold for a count of five and exhale through your mouth. You can stand or sit — it does not matter.

2. Metaphysicians have always used the color white to symbolize protection. It repels all negativity. After three deep breaths, imagine you are surrounded by a brilliant white light. If it helps, think of yourself inside an egg.

3. Imagine you are wrapping and surrounding yourself in white light completely around your entire body. Front and back too.

4. Keep breathing deeply and focusing on this white light. Use your power of concentration to create the image and hold it. Use your will power to believe that you are protected in a shield of positive energy that cannot be penetrated by any negativity.

5. Hold the image for a few minutes and then open your eyes.

This is one exercise that will convince you once you try it. You will not believe how calm and relaxed you will be amid a chaotic or intimidating situation. You will remain empowered and not feel drained or exhausted when it is over. Use this exercise before you fall asleep at night. It only takes a few minutes and will make a dramatic difference. Instead of opening your eyes when you are done, allow yourself to drift into a peaceful sleep.

Once you become proficient at this exercise, you can will the white light to surround you in a matter of seconds. You can do this when you begin to feel negativity or when you walk into a situation that is getting ugly and you want to keep strong and remain empowered.

KEY POINTS FOR LIFE SURFING

Life surfers don't hold onto the pain from the past. It's depressing and weighs them down. They learn from their mistakes from the bad rides, but let go of the trauma and the drama connected to them. They see each new wave as a fresh start.

- Lots of folks use natural supplements to keep them fit.

- It is harder to keep your balance and stay on the board if your legs are not strong.

- "Pavlov's advice on how to succeed – Passion and gradualness. Even in those areas where we have already developed a high degree of skill, it sometimes helps to drop back, lower our sights a bit, and practice with a feeling of ease. This is especially true when one reaches a sticking point in progress, where effort for additional progress is unavailing." Ivan Pavlov

- "Continually straining beyond the sticking point is likely to develop undesirable feeling habits of strain, difficulty, and effort." Maxwell Martz

"What things soever ye desire, when ye pray, believe that ye receive them, and ye shall have them." Mark 11:24

14. MAKE THINGS HAPPEN

If we attract the same energy we transmit, then learning to transmit positive energy during times of uncertainty will help us remain mentally and emotionally empowered. A great way to do this is to use the power of prayer.

There is no religious practice so generally accepted yet so little understood as prayer. Most of us have a story to tell about receiving an answer to prayer. Through the years, it has been thought that only the will of God has much to do with the outcome of prayer requests. What many people do not know is that there are universal laws of metaphysics in place which must be understood in order to fully utilize the power of prayer.

In most cases, prayer is a petition placed before a person who is presumed to be in a position to grant it. Since most of our prayers are for physical or material aid, it is like asking our parents for what we want. Sometimes we get it and sometimes not, but we may never know why or have the understanding or confidence to set out to obtain these things on our own.

The true power of prayer lies in your ability to rise above your dependencies upon others. Using the exercises for concentration and to strengthen your energy will enable you to focus your attention upon your goal while ridding yourself of unwanted inhibitions and thoughts. Your appeal for material things should have you tap into external levels of energy, which is not a hit or miss method, but one that is unselfish.

A wonderful story about the power of prayer comes from Chronicles 20 in the Old Testament of the Bible. Jehoshaphat, the king of Judea, was facing war with the Moabites, Ammonites, and some of the Meunites. The armies of Ammon, Moab, and Mount Seir were heading towards Jerusalem. All the people of Judea came together in Jerusalem to seek solace and comfort from the Lord. Jehoshaphat responded by addressing the assembly of Judea at the temple of the Lord.

Jehoshaphat told his people that the Lord rules over all kingdoms and nations. Power is in His hands and no one can withstand His might. He said that if calamity came upon them, whether by sword, judgment, plague, or famine, they will stand in the Lord's presence in this temple, and cry out to Him in their distress and He will hear and save them.

Jehoshaphat spoke to the Lord and told him the people of Judea were awarded the land of Israel by his hand and they were forbidden to invade the territories of Ammon, Moab, and Mount Seir. Jehoshaphat asked the Lord why he was not judging them for coming to drive the people of Judea out of the land the Lord had given them. He confessed to the Lord that his people had no power to stop the vast army that was approaching, but that they would keep their faith in his power.

All the people of Judea were gathered listening to Jehoshaphat when the spirit of the Lord came upon Jahazziel, the son of Zechariah. Jahazziel spoke to the king and said that the Lord does not want the people of Judea to be afraid or discouraged. The battle was not theirs but the Lord's. Jahazziel said to march down against the enemies the next day, but not to fight the battle. Jahazziel told them to take up their positions, stand firm, and watch the deliverance the Lord will give them. His message was to go out the next day and, instead of being afraid and discouraged, have faith that the Lord will be with them.

Upon hearing the words from Jahazziel, Jehoshaphat fell to his knees with his face to the ground, and all the people of Judea followed, giving praise to the Lord.

The next morning, they left for the desert of Tekoa and, as they set out, Jehoshaphat told his people to have faith in the Lord and they would be victorious. He then appointed men to sing to the Lord and praise Him for the splendor of His holiness as they went out to face the vast armies in the desert.

As they began to sing and praise, the Lord set ambushes against the armies of Ammon, Moab, and Mount Seir, and they were defeated. The men of Ammon and Moab rose up against the army of Mount Seir and destroyed them. Then they turned against each other and annihilated one another.

Then, led by Jehoshaphat, all the men of Judea retuned to Jerusalem to rejoice and give praise to the Lord. The fear of God came upon all the kingdoms of the countries when they heard how the Lord had fought against the enemies of Israel.

This story has several meanings. One is that there are times when we are faced with adversity too large for us to handle. Turning to our faith in prayer helps us reach deeper inside for the strength and conviction to continue, even when we feel hopeless. Turning to prayer also helps us focus on something else besides the enormous task in front of us. Instead of allowing ourselves to continue to feel the fear and negativity of the reality of the situation, we change to feeling more positive and hopeful about it. Once we shift our feelings, we shift our energies. This enables us to transmit positive energy, which in turn attracts positive results.

This was illustrated in the story of Jehoshaphat.

Positive energy is always stronger than negative, and prayer is a way to turn our negativity around. When people are in transition and going through challenging times of change, old prayer methods may not always bring them the results they want. They may be called to look into other cultures or religions for prayer methods, or to stretch beyond their understanding of prayer.

As a general rule, prayer is a communion with God. It is a response to a Higher Power which calls us to still our minds and to listen. Different methods work for different people, so don't be afraid to try something new to see how it works for you.

The power of prayer can be compared to baking a cake. You need flour, water, milk, eggs, butter, and flavoring. Even with all the ingredients, you will not have a cake unless you know what to do with them and when to do it. When you know this and how to mix everything in the right proportions and in the proper sequence, the resulting batter must be baked. Here you need to know the right amount of heat and the length of time for baking. If the heat is too hot, the cake will burn. If not hot enough, it will be flat and doughy. Therefore, there is a lot more that goes into baking a cake than knowing the ingredients.

To understand the ingredients of the power of prayer, it is essential you know how to tap into the potential of your mind. Nearly everyone's mind becomes cluttered with rambling thoughts. You must be able to clear your mind, focus on the one thought you want, and then let go of it. To learn to do this, we will build on to the exercises we have already done.

1. Sit comfortably in a chair and close your eyes. Do not try this lying in a bed until you have developed your mental discipline, because you will fall asleep.

2. Now begin to relax your physical body. Begin by focusing on your toes. Stay with this thought until you begin to feel them tingle. Once they do, move your thought to your ankles. Again, hold your thought until your ankles begin to tingle. Then move your thought to your calves, knees, thighs, hips, stomach, lower back, upper back, chest, shoulders, arms, hands, neck, face, and head. This will take about three to four minutes, and when you are done, your body will feel limp but your mind will be alert and awake.

3. Now imagine that there is a blank movie screen two inches away from and above your forehead. All you can see is this blank movie screen in front of you.

4. Now fill this screen with a detailed picture of what you want to manifest. See it as a final result. This will require you to remained focused and not waver in your thoughts. You must concentrate on what you are doing. It may not happen the first time you try this exercise, but be patient and keep practicing. The more you practice, the better you will get at visualizing exactly what you want.

5. Once you have created a detailed picture, see the screen become smaller and then disappear. Then focus once again on your body. Begin to move your fingers and toes to bring the feeling back to your body. The more you move them, the more you will feel yourself becoming physically awake. Then, when you are ready, open your eyes.

6. You will feel groggy at first, but this feeling goes away very rapidly. You will feel relaxed and refreshed.

The art of mental creating which I described here is an act of your mind directing energy towards a certain objective. This alone is not enough. The last universal law of metaphysics I will offer is the most important of them all. It states that love is the highest and strongest power. The feeling you feel for a loved one is nearest to the sensation you experience from this energy. It is not physical love, but much more refined. Because it is a definite energy, it should be visualized as the color pink, the color of your heart.

The power of loving energy is like food. It nourishes us and, since like energies attract like energies, when you visualize it, only good comes from it. Let's take the visualization exercise I just offered to its final stage.

1. Sit in a chair in a place where you will not be disturbed.

2. Close your eyes and create a feeling of love and warmth in your heart. Concentrate on an experience or person where love is pervasive. Let this feeling fill your entire body. It's alright if you feel yourself smile.

3. Begin to visualize this loving feeling as a glowing ball of pink light. If you do not see it, then continue to feel it or just know that it is there. It does not matter as long as you know that the ball of pink light is there.

4. Then begin to see the detailed picture of your desired outcome created in prayer.

5. Assert the power of your will and encircle this picture in this pink light. Feel love for this picture and every person who may be involved with its outcome.

6. Hold the image for several minutes. Then release the picture from your mind with the conviction that "it is done."

The preceding two exercises used creative visualization. Here are a few more exercises that are a bit different.

A centering prayer is based on Eastern traditions and gained a great deal of popularity in the 1970s with transcendental meditation. Many faith traditions in the West have also used centering prayer over the centuries, and the popularity of transcendental meditation drew many faiths back to their contemplative roots. With a centering prayer, you sit quietly and use a prayer word to still your mind. The prayer word should be meaningful to you and could be a simple as God, love, or peace.

Allow yourself to sit quietly and relax by closing your eyes and begin to repeat the prayer word over and over in your mind. If you prefer, you can say it out loud. Try to match saying the word to your breathing. If you become distracted, focus on saying the word. Try this for about five to ten minutes and then gently open your eyes.

Prayer can be done with your hands, using rhythmic, repetitive work such as cross stitch, scrubbing, sawing, or painting a prayer. A meditative thought or word can be used with each brush stroke or stitch, focusing your mind and creating a tangible connection to the Higher Power.

I said earlier that you had to let go of your thoughts in prayer. I also stated several universal laws of metaphysics. This is where they merge. Since everything is energy, and energy follows thought, you now have to act on the visualization to make it happen. Your motto now needs to be, "If it is meant to be, it is up to me!"

You know what you want. You can create a plan of action to get you there. You have techniques for dealing with difficult people and developing strategies to build rapport with people who are different from you. You can begin to work on developing the mental discipline to block out distractions and gain strength when you feel tired and drained. The power of prayer will enable you to tap into the potential of your mind and utilize energy to help manifest your desires. It will also make sure you keep your energy positive and attract only positive experiences back to you.

KEY POINTS FOR LIFE SURFING

Life surfers are willing to look beyond themselves for help and support. They set their ego aside and realize there are greater powers beyond themselves.

- Surfers are always praying for great surfing conditions.

- I remember reading in The Wild Tiger that life is like a wild tiger. You can either lie down and let it lay its paw on your head, or sit on its back and ride it.

- " A prayer is to be said

  When the world has gotten you down

  And you feel rotten

  And you are too doggone tired to pray

  And you're in a big hurry and besides you are mad at everyone"
  – Margaret Guenther from The Practice of Prayer

- "The divinest things — religion, love, truth, beauty, justice — seem to lose their meaning and value when we sink into lassitude and indifference. It is a signal that we should quit meditation and books and go out into the open air, into the presence of nature, into the company of flocks and children, where we may drink new health and vigour from the clear and full-flowing fountains of life, afar from the arid wastes of theory and speculation; where we may learn again it is not by intellectual questioning, but by believing, hoping, loving, and doing that man finds joy and peace." John Lancaster Spalding

"Each player must accept the cards life deals him or her. But once they are in hand, he or she alone must decide how to play the cards in order to win the game." Voltaire

15. RECOVERING FROM DEVASTATION

So far, this book has been largely preventative in nature to help us deal with both unexpected and expected waves of change we face in our lives. Now is the time to talk about what to do when a big wave hits and throws everything in our lives into disarray.

Nothing is harder in our lives than coping with a loss that changes our life forever. Daniel's story in the first chapter of this book is a good example. There are many others.

No parent wants to lose a child. No one on their wedding day thinks about divorce, but it happens. The pain and suffering that occurs when someone is told they have cancer, diabetes, or multiple sclerosis is overwhelming.

These are heartbreaking events that leave us groping for answers. They will change our lives forever and usually start a ripple effect of more changes stemming from the initial blast. When a wave of devastation hits, it seems like we will never recover. Sometimes it is so unexpected that it takes awhile for us be able to deal with it. These waves throw us into a phase where we feel lost and unsure. It can often lead to depression and a sense of helplessness.

All of a sudden what was, no longer is. It is the dying of the old and the beginning of the new. We suffer the death of a child, loss of a relationship or loss of a job, changes caused by illness, and our way of life is never the same.

After a wave of devastation hits, we are thrown into a phase of transformation. We, as well as our lives, will never be the way they were. We know we are not what we were, but do not know what we are becoming. We know we are changing, but into what?

I call this time the metamorphosis phase, because symbolically we are like a caterpillar in the cocoon. We can feel ourselves changing from a caterpillar into another form, but it is too dark for us to see what's happening. We feel confined within the cocoon and it is very uncomfortable. The metamorphosis is at times painful and we become impatient. We want this to end now so that we can regain some sense of normalcy.

When you are in the metamorphosis phase, it is not the time to make rash decisions or long-term plans. You may be in shock and feel a sense of numbness. Once you collect yourself, you will see that it is the ending of the old and the beginning of the new, but you are not there yet. You think that for some unexplained reason, this has happened to you and you cannot make it go away.

During this difficult time, many people look to God's will for their path to understanding, others look within themselves for understanding, and still others put blame on other people or circumstances. Regardless of our means of coping, there are stages we all go through before we regain a sense of wholeness.

In her work, *On Death and Dying,* Elizabeth Kubler Ross speaks of five stages individuals and their families go through when confronting the news of imminent death. I have adapted them to provide support when these waves hit.

Stage One is **denial**. How many times have you said, "This cannot be happening. Not to me."? Denial is our way to save face. It is our only sense of self-security. If we don't admit to ourselves or others what happened, we can keep our sense of reality. We keep trying to justify that the change did not happen and there must be some mistake.

When it finally dawns on us that this has happened to us, we then move to Stage Two (**anger**) where we begin to ask, "Why me?" The feeling of denial is replaced with anger, rage, envy, and resentment. We question why this did not happen to someone else. We ask what we did to deserve this. People in our lives may find it difficult to deal with us when we are in Stage Two. We displace our anger onto them and are just plain miserable to be around. Nothing is good enough for us and we become grumpy and demanding.

Stage Three (**bargaining**) usually lasts a short time and has us trying to find ways to postpone the inevitable. We internally bargain with God or the powers that be, saying that if we can get our health, job, or significant other back, we will be a better person. Another form of bargaining is for us to shut the stable door after the horses have left. An example of this is bargaining to quit smoking after being diagnosed with lung cancer, in hopes that the cancer will go away.

Once we are faced with nothing else but having to face our change, we are then hit with a feeling of great loss. **Depression** is Stage Four and has us face our reality. Due to the deterioration of our lives, we face the enormity of what we have lost, what we were, and what we still have to face. We now feel the true effect of the ripple waves and know there is no fight left in us to make things the way they were.

The last stage is **acceptance**. Although we still may not be happy about the changes, we generate the stamina to push on and face the future. We can go through these stages a number of times and in various orders during our metamorphosis.

When the wave of devastation hits us, part of our life is destroyed and gone forever. What was normal suddenly becomes abnormal. The process we go through with these stages allows us to accept the abnormal as the new norm.

When we attempt to deny our new reality, it can lead to panic. As we resist, we devote our energy to what we don't want. The more we fight, we project hostile energy and it draws the same back to us. The more we fight, the more we add additional ripple waves.

Acceptance may be the best approach when faced with the types of loss and devastation discussed in this chapter. When Daniel and I met, he expressed to me that he was bleeding and couldn't make it stop. As we spoke, I asked him to shift his energy to be more positive by looking at where he is resisting or harboring negative feelings. Negative feelings create negative energy, which attracts more negative energy. No one can do this but Daniel himself, and until he can shift his energy, he will continue to bleed.

Acceptance allows us to detach ourselves from the negative energies associated with change and keep our energy strong. Acceptance draws positive energy when we stop looking to place blame and instead make strides to play the hand we have been dealt.

Acceptance stills our mind and heart and moves us away from being preoccupied with vengeance, retaliation, hostility, or fear. When we are devoid of these, we will find it easier to focus and follow the techniques provided in this book. Finding acceptance does not mean that we surrender our self-control. Instead, by detaching from the pain and suffering of our loss, we can keep our energy clean and strong so we can use the steps of the "CHARM" process. We are still in our metamorphosis, but a lot closer to breaking out and becoming a beautiful butterfly.

As a caterpillar we moved slowly and could only crawl. As a butterfly, we soar above the ground as a beauty of nature. The metamorphosis phase is never easy for any of us. We've all heard that when one door shuts, another opens. Once we reach acceptance, we shift to more positive energy, which draws opportunity. We are closer to knowing who we are becoming and what we want and don't want moving forward.

When we reach this point, it is very cathartic to get rid of what we no longer want. This can be done physically, mentally, and emotionally. As an example, we go through our homes and throw away what we no longer need. Cleaning our homes is symbolic for cleaning out our lives.

There is a technique you can use that will help you detach from your negative thoughts and emotions and find acceptance. It is designed to help yourself detach from a past experience or relationship. This is wonderful technique to use if you are harboring negative thoughts or emotions towards someone no longer in your life. It even works if the person is deceased and you did not have the chance to express yourself to him or her.

- Think of what is it you want to say to this person.

- Then write it down on a piece of paper. Keep writing until you have said everything you need to say. Put all your emotions into it, even it makes you angry or want to cry.

- Once you are done, do not read it.

- Instead, either rip it up or place in a safe place and burn it.

- Once the paper is destroyed, your connection to this person will be changed forever. Do not keep thinking about the relationship in the same way. Know that your words were heard and you are free to go about your life without any more guilt, anger, or hostility towards this person. Your energy is clean and positive towards this person.

You can do this if you feel negative about anything in your life, past or present. Still harboring anger towards that boss who fired you five years ago? How about the time you worked so hard on a work project and someone else got all the credit? I think you get the idea. Instead of keeping these negative thoughts and emotions buried inside you, use this technique to bring them to light and detach from them.

It's not easy to shift your energy. A few months ago, I was told that my job was being relocated to the West Coast. It came as a complete shock because I felt pretty secure in my job and had been with this company for over twelve years. In one five-minute call, that all changed, as I knew that I was not in a position to relocate and had no choice but to leave the company.

After hearing the news, I was immediately faced with dealing with my issues regarding safety and security. I went through denial pretty quickly and realized the inevitable. I then got angry for a day, but then faced the choice I would have to make. I could both wallow in self-pity and continue to resist this change, or embrace and accept it. I still was not sure what I was going to do, but I knew that staying in my old job was not an option.

Instead of trying to decide what I wanted to do with my career, I began to think about what I did not want to do. I made a list and eliminated everything I knew I could not or would not do. That made it easier for me to decide what direction I wanted to go, and once I knew that, I could apply the "CHARM" process to get me there.

Over the next few months, I dedicated my energies to writing this book and opened a consulting practice. I was proactive and made the effort to reach out and make contacts for finding work. Having a clear focus, a plan, and strong positive energy made things happen. Now, work seems to come my way the more I look for it.

People I talk to are amazed that I made so much progress in such a short amount of time. Although I appreciate their comments, I have not done anything anyone else cannot do. By following the same processes discussed in this book, I let go of my past and opened the door to the next step in my life.

Instead of sitting on the beach, wallowing in my self-pity, I grabbed my board and went riding. Although I did not like some of waves I rode at first, I began to find better ones and keep finding more.

KEY POINTS FOR LIFE SURFING

There is always the risk of a wipeout. No one enjoys the pain and suffering associated with them. Life can be very cruel and unforgiving. Life surfers won't let the hard times deter them. They pick themselves up, dust themselves off, and adopt a resilient nature. They never forget the pain — they use it to burn their fire of inspiration.

- Live for one wave at a time.

- Accept hardship as the way to mastery.

- When the wave gets rough, trust and surrender to the will of the wave.

- "God grant me the serenity to accept the things I cannot change, the courage to change the things I can, and the wisdom to know the difference." The Serenity Prayer by Reinhold Niebuhr

"When you're ripe you rot, when you're green you grow." Enid Hoffman

16. PUTTING IT ALL TOGETHER

We all want the best for ourselves. We want our lives to be full of good experiences. We also know that life will not always go the way we want. At times, it gives us rewards for the work we do, and other times disappointments that, if looked at in a positive light, become opportunities for growth.

Each of us has all sorts of ideas and convictions about ourselves and the world around us that bear no relation to the real facts. We make attempts to clear away some of our illusions, and the hardest person to see and understand is ourselves. Self-deception is the most common of all deceptions, and most of us grow old fondly believing that we are good and lovable beings and the rest of the world is wrong.

It is not easy to break through the walls of self-approval you build around yourself, but if you are ever to realize, even to a small degree, the great potential you possess, certain clarity of vision and understanding is essential.

Do not take things for granted. Use the techniques and ideas offered in this book. The sooner you act, the sooner you will make positive changes in your life. You will take control and direct yourself towards what you desire. Use your mind to appraise and evaluate the information in this book. Apply your energy to practice the exercises.

As you create a better personal world for yourself, you will create more opportunity and freedom for your personal power. Wield this power wisely and you will bring satisfaction to you and to those around you. Your enthusiasm for life will be contagious. Your radiance will be evident to others and others will seek you out for your advice and wisdom.

We learn by doing, so I encourage you not to waste any time. If you want to discover how to tap into your untapped potential, become a great life surfer, and create the life you want, do it now! Practice the exercises and use them. No one will do this for you. The process is in this book. It has been proven to work for thousands, so why not you? The pace of your evolution is now up to you.

I believe we have the power to manifest what we want, in the way we want, in our lives. We just need to learn how to get out of our own way and use our power for us, not against us. To do this takes courage, dedication, and stamina.

I do not profess to have all the right answers for how to do this. No one does. I do know that becoming a good life surfer works. Just when I think my life is going great, it twists or turns in another direction. It always seems that I am faced with challenges for my family, career, or money. To keep my balance, I use my Life Surfing skills and accept these as lessons to learn on my way to mastering life.

I hate being bored. I can't imagine what my life would be like if it remained constant. I relish the challenge of new things. I never look forward to loss and devastation, but I know that is a part of life. I accept that I have gone through and will keep going through death cycles many times. Each time brings me to the next step in my life.

My strategy is to cope with the bad times in a way to keep the damage minimal. I have been called the eternal optimist by many because I seldom let myself stay down for long. I go through my mourning process quickly and move on. I believe that if I lose something and it is meant to be in my life, it will come back. Perhaps in a different form, but nonetheless, it will come back. If something is not meant to be in my life, then it will be replaced with something better. Perhaps at the time I might not think that what I received is better than what I had, but over time, it has always worked out to be better.

Over the last twenty-five years, I have become more spiritual in my quest for self-awareness. I continue my studies to quench my thirst for knowledge. It is very satisfying that my energy has rubbed off on many of the people I have met through my seminars and training classes. Their inspiration was a catalyst for my writing this book. Our sharing of ideas and time together has opened my mind and heart to new ways of living our lives. My hope is that this book has done the same for you.

APPENDIX A

THE "CHARM" PROCESS

C = CONCENTRATE

H = HAVE A PLAN

A = ALIGN YOUR ENERGY

R = RESTRUCTURE YOUR RELATIONSHIPS

M = MAINTAIN YOUR POWER

Here are all the exercises that were provided in this book. They are categorized by title and some of them will have additional applications for your use.

Mental Discipline Exercises

1. When you go into a room for the first time, shut your eyes for a second and see how many objects in the room you can identify. Are there tables, chairs, furniture, or pictures? What are the colors of the walls? Do this whenever you enter a new room.

2. Buy a box of stick matches. Dump them on a table. Put them back in the box with the match heads facing the same way. Then dump them again. Now put them back with every third match head facing the other way.

3. In the evening, try to recall what you ate for breakfast. What you did you do when you first left the house or after breakfast? What did you first see after leaving the house or eating breakfast? What did you do? Spend about three or four minutes on this activity, no more. The next day, recall what you did after lunch. Do this exercise for any three- or four-minute period of your day.

4. Do you have steps in your home? If so, you use them many

times during the day. Do you know how many steps there are? When you use them, you are always thinking about something else. From now on, count each step as you use them. Stay in the present and use the conscious mind when you use your steps.

5. Here is a great exercise to use when you have lost your composure and need to regain your focus. Perhaps you were doing something and got distracted or you are almost ready to give a presentation to a group of fellow employees and you feel nervous and/or distracted. To gain your composure and focus, try counting backwards from 100 using every third number. It goes like this, 100, 97, 94, 91, 88, etc. It does not take long and can be done silently. No one has to know you are even doing it. By the time you get down to single digits, you will have regained composure and your focus. Try doing this four or five times a day. Once you get the hang of it and it becomes familiar, change it to every fourth number. You can also use letters of the alphabet or other sets of numbers. Start at 555 and count backwards using every third number.

6. Multiply in your head any two-digit number by another two-digit number. An example is to multiply 39 x 47. You cannot use your fingers or pen and paper. You can only use your mind. In the beginning, the numbers will jump around, but with practice they will stay in place and you will be able to do this. Once you get the hang of this, try using three-digit numbers.

7. Select someone who is seated five or six rows in front of you. Look at the back of his or her head and imagine them turning around to look at you. If you do this with focus and concentration, the person will turn around. Don't look surprised, just smile at him or her and feel good about your efforts. You can try this exercise almost anywhere - while riding on a bus, on an airplane, or in a movie theater.

8. Listen to a CD, cassette tape, or record of a piece of classical music. Select one instrument and try to follow that instrument through the entire piece. Block out all the other instruments. Just listen to the one you selected. Keep doing this by selecting

another instrument. With practice, in time you will be able to listen selectively to any instrument you focus on. This will help you in two ways. You will have the mental discipline to focus in on conversations that are important, while also having the ability to block out those that are distracting.

9. On a day when there are nice big clouds in the sky, go outside and sit or lie back in the grass. Look up into the sky and pick one cloud. Squint your eyes closed a bit and stare at the middle of the cloud and concentrate on that spot. Maintain your focus and you will begin to see the cloud split exactly where you are focusing. Remain focused for a minute or two. Then look normally and you will see the cloud has split exactly where you were focusing. Not only is this great to enhance your mental discipline, it enforces another universal law of metaphysics, energy follows thought.

10. Begin by lighting a single candle, and place it on a table about five to six feet from you. Sit in a chair, squint your eyes a bit, and concentrate on the flame. Keep looking at the flame and see it get smaller and smaller. Keep concentrating on it. Once you see the flame become small, keep concentrating until it goes out. Once it does, open you eyes fully to see that the flame is no longer lit.

RELAXATION & MEDITATION

1. Sit comfortably in a chair with your weight evenly balanced between your feet. Take a deep breath and count to seven. Breathe through your nose and do not count too fast or too slow, but keep your breathing slow and evenly paced. Hold your breath for a count of seven. As you do this, begin to feel your body relax. Exhale through your mouth for a count of seven and imagine that you are releasing all your stress and anxiety as you exhale.

Each time you inhale, you breathe in new fresh energy. As you hold your breath, you allow this energy to move through your body, breaking up tension within your body. As you exhale, you let go of the tension. While performing this exercise, keep your jaws closed and clench each hand into a fist. Keep the rest of your body except your jaw and hands relaxed. As you breathe in, focus on the energy moving in from the soles of you feet and up through your body. As you hold your breath, focus on the energy moving throughout your entire body. As you exhale, focus on the energy leaving your body.

Perform the inhale, hold, and exhale process seven times. Now that wasn't so bad, was it? It should make your feel great. In fact, it should make you feel so good that within fifteen to twenty minutes, you will feel a surge of energy. It will continue for several hours. You will feel invigorated and alive. This exercise can be used as often as you like. I recommend you practice it once a day. It is great to use after lunch to avert that afternoon sleepy period.

2. Do this exercise in the morning. Stand in front of a window or outdoors, facing the sun, erect and relaxed, with your feet touching and arms extended palms facing up. The sun is our most powerful source of energy. Close your eyes and visualize the sun as this powerful flaming orb of energy. Mentally focus your thoughts on the sun. Feel its warmth upon your skin. Inhale to a count of five and breathe in the energy of the sun. Hold your breath for a count of five and feel the warmth move through your body. As you slowly exhale, breathe out though your mouth and imagine your body surrounded by a large yellow ball of energy. Repeat the breathing process ten times.

MAINTAIN YOUR POSITIVE ENERGY IN ALL YOUR RELATIONSHIPS AND LIFE SITUATIONS

1. Sit comfortably and breathe using the same process described in earlier exercises. Once you are relaxed, focus your concentration on your solar plexus. This is the soft area right below your breast bone. Begin to imagine that with each breath, you take in gold light, and when you exhale, you release a stream of golden light through your solar plexus. Imagine that this beam of light surrounds you, encasing you in an orb of golden light. Each time you breathe, breathe in golden light. Each time you exhale, release it through your solar plexus in a beam of light. The more you breathe, the brighter the orb around you becomes. Now think of a person in your life you no longer like, or perhaps someone you have never liked, but have to live or work with. Imagine they are standing facing you, about ten feet away. Begin to imagine a chord of light between your solar plexus and theirs. Since this relationship has negative energy attached to it, the chord of light will be dark grey. Underneath the grey is gold, but there is too much negative energy to see it. Place both of your hands around this chord of light as if you were holding onto a rope that connects you to this person. Begin to walk toward them, keeping your hands on the chord. As you walk, you wipe away the negative energy with your hands and turn the grey color to gold. Walk all the way to them until you have cleansed the entire chord and it is completely gold. If you wish to break the relationship with this person, or have already done so physically or emotionally, then use your hands like scissors and cut the cord. Although you may still see this person in your life, you no longer have any negative energy attached to the relationship. You can do this for as many people or situations as you like. If you want to maintain the relationship to the person or situation, then do not cut the chord, but make sure it shines brightly in gold. Repeat this exercise again if the relationship or situation becomes negative again.

To keep you empowered when you are in an intimidating situation

Close your eyes and take a deep breath through your nose, hold for a count of five, and exhale through your mouth. You can stand or sit, it does not matter. Metaphysicians have always used the color white to symbolize protection. It repels all negativity. After three deep breaths, imagine you are surrounded by a brilliant white light. If it helps, think of yourself inside an egg.

Imagine you are wrapping and surrounding yourself in white light around your entire body. Front and back too. Keep breathing deeply and focusing on this white light. Use your power of concentration to create the image and hold it. Use your will power to believe that you are protected in a shield of positive energy that cannot be penetrated by any negativity. Hold the image for a few minutes and then open your eyes.

Exercises for Prayer & Manifestation

1. Sit comfortably in a chair. Close your eyes. Do not try this lying in a bed until you have developed your mental discipline, as you will fall asleep. Now begin to relax your physical body. Begin by focusing on your toes. Stay with this thought until you begin to feel them tingle. Once they do, move your thought to your ankles. Again hold your thought until your ankles begin to tingle. Then move your thought to your calves, knees, thighs, hips, stomach, lower back, upper back, chest, shoulders, arms, hands, neck, face, and head. This will take about three to four minutes and when you are done, your body will feel limp but your mind alert and awake. Now imagine that there is a blank movie screen two inches away from and above your forehead. All you can see is this blank movie screen in front of you. Now fill this screen with a detailed picture of what you want to manifest. See it as a final result. This will require you to remain focused and not waver in your thoughts. You must concentrate on what you are doing. It may not happen the first time you try this exercise, but be patient and keep practicing. The more you practice, the better you will get at visualizing exactly what you

want. Once you have created a detailed picture, see the screen become smaller and then disappear. Then focus once again on your body. Begin to move your fingers and toes to bring the feeling back to your body. The more you move them, the more you will feel yourself becoming physically awake. Then when you are ready, open your eyes. You will feel groggy at first, but this feeling goes away very rapidly. You will feel relaxed and refreshed.

2. Sit in a chair in a place where you will not be disturbed. Close your eyes and create a feeling of love and warmth in your heart. Concentrate on an experience or person where love is pervasive. Let this feeling fill your entire body. It's all right if your feel yourself smile. Begin to visualize this loving feeling as a glowing ball of pink light. If you do not see it, then continue to feel it or just know that it is there. It does not matter, as long as you know that the ball of pink light is there. Then begin to see the detailed picture of your desired outcome created. Assert the power of your will and encircle this picture in this pink light. Feel love for this picture and every person who may be involved with its outcome. Hold the image for several minutes. Then release the picture from your mind with the conviction that "it is done."

BIBLIOGRAPHY AND RESOURCES

BIBLIOGRAPHY

"Alcoholics Anonymous" Alcoholics Anonymous World Services Inc., 1976.

Barrow, Terrance. *Captain Cook In Hawaii*. Norfolk Island, Australia: Island Heritage Limited, 1978.

Chan, Wing-Tsit. *A Source Book in Chinese Philosophy*. Princeton, New Jersey: Princeton University Press, 1963.

Finney, Ben. *Surfing: The Sport of Hawaiian Kings*. Rutland, VT: C.E. Tuttle, 1966.

Guenther, Margaret. *The Practice of Prayer*. Boston: Cowley Publications, 2001.

Hayward, Susan. *A Guide for the Advanced Soul*. Avalon, Australia: In-Tune Books, 1984.

_____. *Begin It Now*. Avalon, Australia: In-Tune Books, 1987.

Kampion, Drew. *Stoked, A History of Surf Culture*. Santa Monica, CA: General Publishing Group, 1997.

_____. *The Book of Waves*. Santa Barbara, CA: Arpel/Surfer, 1989.

Kiersey, David & Marilyn Bates. *Please Understand Me*. Del Mar, CA: Prometheus Book Co., 1978.

Kroeger Otto & Janet M. Thuesen. *Type Talk*. New York: Dell Publishing, 1988.

Long, Max Freedom. *Recovering the Ancient Magic*. London: The C.W. Daniel Company, 1936.

_____. *The Secret Science Behind Miracles*. Santa Cruz, CA: DeVorss Publications, 1948.

_____. *The Secret Science at Work*. Santa Cruz, CA: DeVorss Publications, 1983.

Maxwell, John C. *Living at the Next Level*. Nashville, TN: Thomas Nelson, Inc., 1996.

Maslow, Abraham H. *Maslow on Management*. New York: John Wiley & Sons, Inc., 1998.

Moring M.A., Gary. *The Complete Idiot's Guide to Understanding Einstein*. Indianapolis, IN; Alpha Books, 2000.

"Narcotics Anonymous." Van Nuys, CA: World Service Office Inc., 1998.
Ross, Elizabeth Kubler. *On Death and Dying*. New York: Macmillan Publishing Co., Inc., 1969.

RESOURCES

"A Course in Miracles." Farmingdale, NY: Coleman Graphics, 1975.

Connor, Daryl R. *Managing at the Speed of Change*. New York: Villard Books, 1992.

Connor, Daryl R. *Leading at the Edge of Chaos*. New York: John Wiley & Sons, Inc, 1998.

David, Joel. *Mapping the Mind*. Toronto: Carol Publishing Co., 1997.

Gawain, Shakti. *Living in the Light*. Mill Valley, CA: Whatever Publishing Co., 1986.

Isbyam, I.C. *Metaphysics and Modern Research*. London: The C.W. Daniel Company, Ltd. 1927.

Wolinsky, Stephen. *Quantum Consciousness*. Norfolk, CT: Bramble Books, 1993.

Wyschogrod, Edith. *The Phenomenon of Death*. New York: Harper & Row Publishers, 1973.

Zukov, Gary. *The Dancing Wu Li Masters*. New York: William Morrow & Co., Inc., 1980.

About the Author

Norman Mitchell is an Organizational Psychologist with over 25 years experience as a Management and Performance Consultant. His work has focused on improving organizational effectiveness with organizations in the Insurance, Automobile, Banking, Telecommunications, and Manufacturing Industries. Norman has developed and delivered corporate training courses targeted at enhancing Leadership Development, Communication, Crisis and Change Management, and Self-Empowerment Skills.

Norman wrote this book to respond to the many requests he received from participants in his corporate training courses and has integrated the skills used in ocean surfing to create the concept of life surfing, which after 25 years of teaching workshops, seminars, and corporate training classes, are skills that have proven to be extremely successful for addressing times of stress, change, uncertainty, and crisis. Norman's use of life surfing exercises and techniques are a composite of many years of research and study in Psychology, Philosophy, Eastern Religions, Physics, Metaphysics and New Age Methodologies.

You can contact the author at norm.mitchell@verizon.net

Printed in the United States
39727LVS00002B/142-243

9 781420 863826